D0846816

*The thirst for glory is not ended by satisfying it
but rather by extinguishing it.*

Luther, Heidelberg Disputation

On Being a
Theologian of the Cross

Reflections on Luther's
Heidelberg Disputation, 1518

Gerhard O. Forde

WILLIAM B. EERDMANS PUBLISHING COMPANY
GRAND RAPIDS, MICHIGAN / CAMBRIDGE, U.K.

© 1997 Wm. B. Eerdmans Publishing Co.
255 Jefferson Ave. S.E., Grand Rapids, Michigan 49503 /
P.O. Box 163, Cambridge CB3 9PU U.K.

All rights reserved

Printed in the United States of America

02 01 00 99 98 97   7 6 5 4 3 2 1

Library of Congress Cataloging-in-Publication Data

Forde, Gerhard O.
On being a theologian of the Cross: reflections on Luther's
Heidelberg disputation / Gerhard O. Forde.
p.   cm.
Includes bibliographical references.
ISBN 0-8028-4345-X (alk. paper)
1. Luther, Martin, 1483-1546. Disputatio Heidelbergae habita.
2. Luther, Martin, 1483-1546.—Contributions to theology.
3. Atonement. 4. Jesus Christ—Crucifixion. 5. Holy Cross.
6. Religious disputations—Germany. 7. Reformation—Sources.
I. Luther, Martin, 1483-1546. Disputatio Heidelbergae habita.
English. II. Title.
BR332.5.F67 1997
230'.41'092—dc21   97-8591
                                                    CIP

Contents

Preface

I have three reasons for writing this little book. First, to fill a need. Talk about the theology of the cross seems to be growing in church circles, and I am often asked what a theology of the cross is and what makes it so different from other kinds of theology. After I try to give as helpful a reply as I can, which under the circumstances of casual conversation is usually sketchy and superficial, the next question is whether there is something to read that would enlighten further. Then, alas, I am even more at a loss. Even though there is some literature available in German, there isn't much of anything in English one can recommend enthusiastically to the ordinary reader.[1] To be sure, there are works like Walther von Loewenich's *Luther's Theology of the Cross* (Minneapolis: Augsburg, 1976), the classic treatment of the subject that first appeared in German in 1929. It is still essential reading for anyone who wishes to delve deeply into the theology of the cross. However, it is heavy going for

---

1. There has been a recent burgeoning of articles and books concerned with the theology of the cross, but most of it is related to questions surrounding liberation theology or problems of victimization, speculation about the "vulnerability" of God, and so forth, which doesn't get at the central issue of being a theologian of the cross as I attempt to set that forth here.

one not aware of some of the scholarly debates of the time, and it was written as much to make a case about Luther's theological development as it was to expound the theology of the cross per se. More recently, Alister McGrath has also written a book with the same title, *Luther's Theology of the Cross* (Oxford: Basil Blackwell, 1985), but that too, even though well worth reading and helpful, is rather an interpretation of Luther's development than a treatment of the theology of the cross. We thus find ourselves in a situation where there is increasing talk about the theology of the cross but little specific knowledge of what exactly it is. Although this treatise cannot pretend to exhaust the subject, it does hope to make a modest addition to the understanding of the theology of the cross.

The second reason I have for writing follows from the first. In the absence of clear understanding, the theology of the cross tends to become sentimentalized, especially in an age that is so concerned about victimization. Jesus is spoken of as the one who "identifies with us in our suffering," or the one who "enters into solidarity with us" in our misery. "The suffering of God," or the "vulnerability of God," and such platitudes become the stock-in-trade of preachers and theologians who want to stroke the psyche of today's religionists. But this results in rather blatant and suffocating sentimentality. God is supposed to be more attractive to us because he identifies with us in our pain and suffering. "Misery loves company" becomes the unspoken motif of such theology.

A theology of the cross, however, is not sentimentalism. To be sure, it speaks much about suffering. A theologian of the cross, Luther says, looks at all things through suffering and the cross. It is also certainly true that in Christ God enters into our suffering and death. But in a theology of the cross it is soon apparent that we cannot ignore the fact that suffering comes about because we are at odds with God and are trying to rush headlong into some sort of cozy identification with him. God and his Christ, Luther will be concerned to point out, are the *operators* in the matter, not the ones operated upon (thesis 27, Heidelberg Disputation). In the gospel of John, Jesus is concerned to point out that no one takes his life from him but that he lays it down of his own accord (John 10:18). In the end, Jesus suffers and dies because *nobody* identified with him. The people cried, "Crucify him!" One of his disciples betrayed him, another denied him, the rest forsook him and fled. He died alone, forsaken even by God.

Now we in turn *suffer* the absolute and unconditional working of God upon us. It is a suffering because as old beings we cannot abide such working. We are rendered *passive* by the divine activity. "Passive," it should be remembered here, comes from the same root as "passion," which is, of course, "to suffer." And so we look on the world anew in the light of Christ's Passion, "through suffering and the cross" (thesis 20), as ones who suffer the sovereign working of God. A sentimentalized theology gives the impression that God in Christ comes to join us in our battle against some unknown enemy, is victimized, and suffers just like us. Like the daughters of Jerusalem we sympathize with him. A true theology of the cross places radical question marks over against sentimentality of that sort. "Weep not for me," Jesus said, "but for yourselves and for your children."

My third reason for writing is related to the second. It is evident that there is a serious erosion or slippage in the language of theology today. Sentimentality leads to a shift in focus, and the language slips out of place. To take a common example, we apparently are no longer sinners, but rather victims, oppressed by sinister victimizers whom we relentlessly seek to track down and accuse. Of course, there are indeed victims and victimizers in our culture — all too many of them. But the kind of collective paranoia that allows us to become preoccupied with such a picture of our plight cannot help but nudge the language just enough to cause it to slip and fall out of place. The slippage is often very slight and subtle and hardly noticeable; that is what makes it so deceptive.

We no longer live in a guilt culture but have been thrown into meaninglessness — so we are told. Then the language slips out of place. Guilt puts the blame on us as sinners, but who is responsible for meaninglessness? Surely not we! Sin, if it enters our consciousness at all, is generally something that "they" did to us. As Alan Jones, Dean of the Episcopal Cathedral of San Francisco, put it once, "We live in an age in which everything is permitted and nothing is forgiven."

Since we are victims and not really sinners, what we need is affirmation and support, and so on. The language slips and falls out of place. It becomes therapeutic rather than evangelical. It must be trimmed more and more so as not to give offense. In thesis 21 of the Heidelberg Disputation Luther says that a theologian of the cross "says what a thing is," whereas a theologian of glory calls the bad good and the good bad. This stakes out the claim that language and its proper use in matters theological is a fundamental concern of the theologian of the cross. Luther's words suggest that the misuse or slippage of language in this regard has a theological root. When we operate on the assumption that our language must constantly be trimmed so as not to give offense, to stroke the psyche rather than to place it under attack, it will of course gradually decline to the level of greeting-card sentimentality. The language of sin, law, accusation, repentance, judgment, wrath, punishment, perishing, death, devil, damnation, and even the cross itself — virtually one-half of the vocabulary — simply disappears. It has lost its theological legitimacy and therefore its viability as communication.

A theologian of the cross says what a thing is. In modern parlance: a theologian of the cross calls a spade a spade. One who "looks on all things through suffering and the cross" is constrained to speak the truth. The theology of the cross, that is to say, provides the theological courage and the conceptual framework to hold the language in place. It will, no doubt, also involve critical appraisal of the language and its use. It will recognize indeed that the half of the vocabulary that has disappeared can be frightening and offensive.

But it will see precisely that the cross and the resurrection itself is the only answer to that problem, not erasure or neglect. So this study hopes to make some small contribution to holding the language in place.

It is curious that in spite of attempts to avoid offense, matters don't actually seem to improve. We seek affirmation, but we seem to experience less and less of it. We look for support, but others are too busy looking for it themselves to pay us much mind. Preachers try to prop up our self-esteem with optimistic blandishments, but more and more people seem to suffer from a deteriorating sense of self-worth. Perhaps a return to calling a spade a spade has its place. At least that is one of the hopes behind this treatise.

This is not to say, however, that the language of affirmation, comfort, support, building self-esteem, and so forth does not have its place. On the level of human relations it can be quite necessary and beneficial. It has its place, however, among that which is penultimate, in caring for the well-being of persons *in this age.* The danger and misuse comes when such language displaces or obscures the ultimate. It would be as though an alcoholic were to confuse breaking the habit with salvation. Penultimate cures are mistaken for ultimate redemption. When that happens the church becomes predominantly a support group rather than the gathering of the body of Christ where the word of the cross and resurrection is proclaimed and heard. This temptation is abroad in the land and must be resisted.

Even though the reasons for wanting to write a treatise on the theology of the cross may be stated, we soon run into the difficult question of how to do it. We discover why there is not much literature available. It is a hard thing, indeed a risky thing, to write about. That will no doubt become clear to the reader here. What is, after all, the subject matter of a theology of the cross? Is it simply a repetition of the Passion story? Hardly. Is it then perhaps just another treatment of the doctrine of atonement? Not really. Is it just an account of an unusual sort of religious experience, a kind of spirituality, as we might say today? That may be closer to the truth, but still not exactly. It is rather a particular perception of the world and our destiny, what Luther came to call looking at all things through suffering and the cross. It has to do with what he referred to often as the question of *usus,* the way the cross is put to use in our lives.

Yet that is rather difficult to write about. Indeed, as I shall maintain later, "a," or "the" theology of the cross cannot really be written. Luther himself does not write a theology of the cross. Rather, particularly in the Heidelberg Disputation, he gives an account of what those who have been smitten and raised up through the event of the cross *do.* In casting about for a way to proceed, therefore, it gradually became clear to me first of all that I should give the work the title *On Being a Theologian of the Cross.* Second, I found that the more I worked with the sources, the more I was drawn to the Heidelberg Disputation itself as an account of what a theologian of the cross does. That is, the Disputation itself is the doing of a theologian of the cross. It is, we might say, what the theologian of the cross puts up for "dispute" before the world. The more I studied that ancient dispute, the more it became evident to me that, in spite of the fact that it is couched in the language and problematic of the 16th century, it is so radical and deep for its time that it is still vital for our time. Because of this radicalness, it anticipates and answers the questions that are with us yet, and no doubt always will be. However, the Disputation in the end needs no apology, not even in appeals to contemporary relevance. Its theology is of such consequence as to command our attention for its own sake. Contemplating it with some care is a theological experience in itself. It leads us to see theological matters in a new light — what Luther meant when he said a theologian of the cross "says what a thing is." So it became clear to me in the end that the form my work should take would be simply some reflections on the

Disputation itself, probing the theses and their proofs as a beginning attempt at opening up the text. It is by no means an exhaustive treatment, but an attempt.

If I have reasons for wanting to write of being a theologian of the cross, I also have some apprehensions. It might well be asked whether there is need or place for theologians of the cross today. They, as we shall see, cannot but appear very critical and negative over against the optimism of a theology of glory. Is it not cruel to attack what little optimism we are able to muster these days? Would not the attack already be too late? The attack in the Heidelberg Disputation begins by ruthlessly shredding all ideas of the place of good works in the scheme of salvation. Yet, as the oft-repeated remark has it, who is trying to do good works any more? Is the theology of the cross a magnificent attack on a nonexistent enemy, a marvelous cure for a disease that no one has? Could it be perhaps, as with smallpox vaccine, that finally the vaccination causes more illness than the disease? Is a theologian of the cross a curious historical relic spreading pessimism where desperate people are hanging on by their fingertips?

We should hesitate, no doubt, to be drawn too easily into arguments about the worth or usefulness of our own efforts. The treatise itself will have to argue its own case. Nevertheless, some preliminary indication of how my apprehensions were set aside long enough to risk writing may be of interest to the reader. In the first place, anyone who gets some glimpse of what it means to be a theologian of the cross immediately realizes that the bane of a theology of glory never vanishes. It is the perennial theology of the fallen race. We have to persist in a theology of the cross in order precisely to expose that fact. In the second place, I laid my apprehension aside because I have come to wonder if the very theology of glory is not in a state of severe crisis. If it is true that no one is trying anymore, what does that portend? Does it mean, as a postmodernist might say, that the "Holy Words" no longer signify a meaningful destiny? Have we lost the thread of the story? Is the "official optimism of North America," as Douglas John Hall spoke of it,[2] finally running off into sand? Could that be one of the reasons for the despair and chaos in our homes and in our streets? Has the thirst for glory finally issued in the despair that Luther foresaw? This treatise is written with the suspicion that the malaise of the theology of glory is the ultimate source of contemporary despair, not the theology of the cross. My writing proceeds on the assumption that a theology of the cross brings hope, indeed, the only ultimate hope.

2. *Lighten Our Darkness* (Philadelphia: Westminster, 1976) and other works. Hall has consistently been one of the most outspoken advocates for a theology of the cross in contemporary theology.

Introductory Matters

Crux sola est nostra theologia.

The cross is in the first instance God's attack on human sin. Of course in the second instance, and finally, it is also salvation from sin. But we miss the bite of it if we do not see that first off it is an attack on sin. Strange attack — to suffer and die at our hands! God's "alien work," Luther called it. As an attack it reveals that the real seat of sin is not in the flesh but in our *spiritual* aspirations, in our "theology of glory." The point is that what happens in the cross[1] is

---

1. The word "cross" here and in the entire treatise that follows is, of course, shorthand for the entire narrative of the crucified and risen Jesus. As such it includes the OT preparation (many of the foundational passages for the theology of the cross come from the OT!), the crucifixion *and* resurrection of Jesus, and his exaltation. It is important to include resurrection and exaltation because there is considerable confusion abroad about their place in a theology of the cross. It is often claimed, for instance, that a theology of glory is a theology of resurrection while a theology of the cross is "only" concerned with crucifixion. Nothing could be further from the truth. As a matter of fact, a theology of the cross is impossible without resurrection. It is impossible to plumb the depths of the crucifixion without the resurrection.

I

completely contradictory to our usual religious thinking. St. Paul knew this. In 1 Corinthians 1:18-25 he said,

> The word of the cross is folly to those who are perishing, but to us who are being saved it is the power of God. For it is written, "I will destroy the wisdom of the wise, and the cleverness of the clever I will thwart." Where is the wise man? Where is the scribe? Where is the debater of this age? Has not God made foolish the wisdom of the world? For since in the wisdom of God the world did not know God through wisdom, it pleased God through the folly of what we preach to save those who believe. For Jews demand signs and Greeks seek wisdom, but we preach Christ crucified, a stumbling block to Jews and folly to Gentiles, but to those who are called, both Jews and Greeks, Christ the power of God and the wisdom of God. For the foolishness of God is wiser than men, and the weakness of God is stronger than men.

Therefore the theology of the cross is an offensive theology. The offense consists in the fact that unlike other theologies it attacks what we usually consider the best in our religion. As we shall see, theologians of the cross do not worry so much about what is obviously bad in our religion, our bad works, as they do about the pretention that comes with our good works. So the theology of the cross can only be spoken of truthfully in contrast to all other types of theology. To express this, Luther made a fundamental distinction between the theology of the cross and the theology of glory. A theology of the cross does not, therefore, present itself as one option among many. In fact, in spite of what seems to be an endless variety of religions and theologies, it would be safe to say from this perspective that there are at the bottom only two types of theology, glory theology and cross theology. "The theology of glory" is a catchall for virtually all theologies and religions. The cross sets itself apart from and over against all of these. It will be one of the purposes of this study to set forth the contrast between these two types of theology as clearly as possible both so that the theology of the cross may be more accurately identified and so that, thereby, the preaching of the cross retains the foolishness that destroys the wisdom of the wise and thus saves even them.

How shall we go about this? As I have already maintained, the theology of the cross is notoriously difficult to write *about*. In fact, it is quite impossible to write "the" or even "a" theology of the cross. The attempt to do so would no doubt be just another attempt to give a final propositional answer to Jesus' cry from the cross, "My God, My God, why have you forsaken me?" We can't answer Jesus' question. We can only die *with him* and await God's answer in him. To claim such an answer would simply be to leave the actual cross behind for the sake of the theology in our books. It would be just another theology *about* the cross, not a theology *of* the cross. Basically all theologies *about* the cross turn out to be theologies of glory.

The difficulty here is that the cross *is* the theo-logy, the logos of God; the word of the cross is the attack. It doesn't coin itself in ready theological propositions that we can appropriate and still go on pretty much as usual. The word of the cross kills and makes alive. It crucifies the old being in anticipation of the resurrection of the new. "The cross alone is our theology,"[2] Luther could say. And those oft-quoted words are to be taken literally. But we cannot fail to notice what an odd claim it is. How can the cross be a theology? The cross is an event. Theology is reflection on and explanation of the event. Theology is *about* the event, is it not? However, that is what makes writing some definitive theology of the cross impossible.

---

2. *CRUX sola est nostra theologia, D. Martin Luthers Werke. Kritische Gesamtausgabe* (Weimarer Ausgabe) (Weimar: Hermann Böhlau, 1883-), 5.176.32. (Hereafter cited as WA.) There is an English translation of the first seven of Luther's *Operationes* in *Luther's Commentary on the First Twenty-two Psalms,* trans. John Nicholas Lenker (Sunbury, Penn.: Lutherans in All Lands Co., 1903), vol. 1. (Herafter cited as Lenker.) The reference here is on page 289.

At best all such theology can do is to clear the way for the proclamation of the cross, to drive us actually to preach the word of the cross as that folly that destroys the wisdom of the wise.

The cross, that is, is not quiescent or dead. The cross is itself in the first instance the attack of God on the old sinner *and the sinner's theology.* The cross is the doing of God to us. But that same cross itself, and only the cross, at the same time opens a new and unheard-of possibility over against the sinner's old self and its theology. That means that a theology of the cross is inevitably quite polemical. It constantly seeks to uncover and expose the ways in which sinners hide their perfidy behind pious facades. The delicate thing about it is that it attacks the *best* we have to offer, not the worst. This explains why the theology of the cross is generally spoken of in contrast to a theology of glory. The two theologies are always locked in mortal combat. Wherever there is mention of a theology of the cross without indication of this combat, it is not truly the theology of the cross that is being expressed. The preacher-theologian must know this and learn how to use the word of the cross in that combat.

The fact that the theology of the cross is always found in combat with the theology of glory and that the preacher-theologian must know how to use the word of the cross in the combat indicates that we might well attempt two things in this introduction before we move to the text of the Heidelberg Disputation itself. First, we shall try to set the background of the combat by a discussion of the two fundamentally different "stories," or, as theologians like to say today, different "narratives," which shape human existence and self-understanding. Second, we shall try to set forth the two different ways of being a theologian that these narratives sponsor. It is hoped that by focusing on the two ways of being theologians we can overcome some of the difficulty inherent in trying to write "about" a theology of the cross. For what such theology seeks to foster is not a competing set of doctrines but, as we shall see, a different way of operating. The goal here is to *become* a theologian of the cross, not merely to talk or write *about* it.

Two Stories: The Glory Story and the Cross Story

The most common overarching story we tell about ourselves is what we will call the glory story. We came from glory and are bound for glory. Of course, in between we seem somehow to have gotten derailed — whether by design or accident we don't quite know — but that is only a temporary inconvenience to be fixed by proper religious effort. What we need is to get back on "the glory road." The story is told in countless variations. Usually the subject of the story is "the soul." Philosophers speak of the soul being trapped in the world of matter, decay, and death through some cosmic misadventure on the part of either the gods or mortals. The basic scheme is what Paul Ricoeur has called "the myth of the exiled soul."[3] The soul is exiled from its home. It is slumbering or has forgotten its way. Its true destiny is to return. The way of return is by knowledge, *gnosis,* the awakening of the soul to its immortal destiny and, consequently, behavior appropriate thereto — which usually means a purging or shucking off of the flesh and its lusts. But through all its variations, the scheme remains pretty much the same: the exile of the soul from the "one" and its return.

The glory story, the myth of the exiled soul, is a powerful story. After all, the dream of the soul's indestructibility is attractive and comforting.

> Tell me not in mournful numbers,
> Life is but an empty dream! —
> For the soul is dead that slumbers
> And things are not what they seem.
>
> Life is real! life is earnest!
> And the grave is not its goal;

3. Paul Ricoeur, *The Symbolism of Evil,* translated by Emerson Buchanan (New York: Harper and Row, 1967), 279ff.

Dust thou art, to dust returnest,
Was not spoken of the soul.[4]

So said Henry Wadsworth Longfellow, the Poet Laureate of American sentimentality, in "A Psalm of Life." Even in a supposedly secular age the myth continues to appeal to basic religious aspirations. The widespread belief in the transmigration of souls and reincarnation among "New Age" religions and such bears witness to that. Indeed, so seductive has the exiled soul myth been throughout history that the biblical story itself has been taken into captivity by it. The biblical story of the fall has tended to become a variation on the theme of the exiled soul.[5] The unbiblical notion of a *fall* is already a clue to that. Adam, originally pure in soul, either by nature or by the added gift of grace was tempted by baser lusts and "fell," losing grace and drawing all his progeny with him into a "mass of perdition." Reparation must be made, grace restored, and purging carried out so that return to glory is possible. The cross, of course, can be quite neatly assimilated into the story as the reparation that makes the return possible. And there we have a tightly woven theology of glory!

This fateful amalgamation of the glory story with the cross story is the hidden presupposition for the deadly combat between the theology of glory and the theology of the cross. Indeed, one of the difficulties in the attempt to set the theology of the cross apart from the theology of glory is that the differences between the two are often very subtle. Obviously they use much the same language in Christian

4. It is interesting how the verses, wittingly or no, mirror the myth. In the myth the "slumber of the soul" is the mark of the "fall" per se. In its slumber, the soul "forgets" the difference between its spiritual nature and the material body in which it is imprisoned. So, exactly, "the soul is dead that slumbers." Salvation comes by awakening. "Dust to dust" cannot, therefore, be a legitimate part of its story.

5. See ibid., 330ff. In his typology Ricoeur speaks of the biblical story as "the Adam myth." What has happened is that the Adam story has been interpreted by the exiled soul story. The "fall" is the story of the "exile" of the soul from its true home.

theological circles. One purpose of this treatise is to attempt to make the differences clearer. The theology of the cross arises out of the realization that it is simply disastrous to dissolve the cross in the story of glory. Jesus was crucified "outside the camp," not in the temple, as the Epistle to the Hebrews tells us. The cross insists on being its own story. It does not allow us to stand by and watch. It does not ask us to probe endlessly for a meaning behind or above everything that would finally awaken, enlighten, and attract the exiled, slumbering soul. The cross draws us into itself so that we become participants in the story. As Paul could put it in Galatians 2:20, "I have been crucified with Christ; it is no longer I who live, but Christ who lives in me; and the life I now live in the flesh I live by faith in the Son of God, who loved me and gave himself for me." Just as Jesus was crucified so we also are crucified with him. The cross makes us part of its story. The cross becomes our story. That is what it means to say, as Luther did, "The cross *alone* is our theology."

This is made quite radically explicit in Luther's little writing, "A Meditation on Christ's Passion,"[6] written about the same time as the Heidelberg Disputation (1519). In that writing Luther is concerned about the proper way to meditate on the Passion of Christ. One does not meditate properly by blaming the Jews, he says, for that only feeds one's antipathy to enemies. Nor does one meditate properly by using Christ's Passion as a kind of exercise or talisman to stave off suffering — wearing crosses and so forth as protection from misfortune. Nor does one meditate properly by pitying and showing sympathy for Jesus, like the daughters of Jerusalem who wept as he went to crucifixion. Rather, "the real and true work of Christ's Passion is to make man conformable to Christ, so that man's conscience is tormented by his sins in like measure as Christ was pitiably tormented in body and soul by our sins. . . .

6. *Luther's Works*, ed. Jaroslav Pelikan and Helmut T. Lehmann (Philadelphia: Fortress Press, 1958-72), 42.7-14. (Hereafter cited as LW.)

Now the whole world closes in upon you. . . ."[7] Conscience can no longer defend us. Luther thus projects for us an inescapable awareness of being drawn into the event:

> You must get this thought through your head and not doubt that you are the one who is torturing Christ thus, for your sins have surely wrought this. . . . Therefore when you see the nails piercing Christ's hands, you can be certain that it is your work. When you behold his crown of thorns, you may rest assured that these are your evil thoughts, etc.[8]

Thus the cross story becomes our story. It presses itself upon us so that it becomes inescapable. It fights to displace the glory story. The cross thereby becomes the key to the biblical story and opens up new possibilities for appropriating — or better, being appropriated by — the entire story. It is no wonder that crucial texts for a theology of the cross over against a theology of glory come from the Old Testament.[9] Indeed, one might say that the so-called Christological interpretation of the OT over which so much scholarly ink has been spilt is in the end nothing but the claim that the OT is "cruciform" in its theology and most certainly not a theology of glory. To be sure, Christological interpretation has too often been done in a simplistic, allegorical fashion, but at the deepest level it is really the attempt to separate out the OT story once again from its contamination by the story of the exiled soul. Indeed, the OT finally comes into its own in the light of a theology of the cross. It is vital to realize that a proper theology of the cross does not isolate attention just on the cross event. To speak of the "cross story" is a shorthand way of intending the entire story

7. LW 42.10.
8. LW 42.9.
9. For instance, Exod. 33:18-23, Deut. 32:39-42, 1 Sam. 2:6-7, the Psalms, especially the penitential and lament psalms, Isa. 28:21; 45; 53, and so forth.

culminating in cross and resurrection. The cross is the key to unlocking the entire story.

Thus the cross story claims us. And we should make no mistake. Unless the cross story does claim us and become our story, we shall not escape the clutches of the glory story. It is not a matter of choice, a matter over which we deliberate. One of the decisive questions in the battle between a theology of glory and a theology of the cross will always be the question of the will. A theology of glory always leaves the will in control. It must therefore seek to make its theology attractive to the supposed "free will." A theology of the cross assumes that the will is bound and must be set free. The cross story does that. Either it claims us or it doesn't. If it does, it is the end of the glory story. We see in the death of Jesus our death, and we remember that we are dust. We can begin to take the truth. We learn dying. Our story is not that of the exit from and return to glory of an undying soul. The cross destroys all that. It "destroys the wisdom of the wise." "Ashes to ashes, dust to dust." That marks the parameters of our story as far as human possibility is concerned. We see, as Luther puts it, the way things really are.[10] We look at all things through "suffering and the cross." We live only on the strength of the fact that the Creator breathed his Spirit into the dust and gave us life. We live on "borrowed time" — time lent us by the Creator. Yet we also see in the death of Jesus on the cross our rebellion against that life, and we note that there is absolutely no way out now except one. God vindicated the crucified Jesus by raising him from the dead. So the question and the hope comes to us. "If we die with him shall we not also live with him?" That is the end of the story — for the time being. But it is the beginning of faith.

10. See below theses 19-21 of the Heidelberg Disputation.

Two Ways of Being a Theologian

The two stories, the glory story and the cross story, join in mortal combat over which shall define and determine our destiny. The cross itself is the place where the combat is joined. When the cross conquers, it becomes clear to us that there is a quite different way of being a theologian. We become a theologian of the cross. Just as there are two basic stories, there are two ways of being a theologian. We are either a theologian of glory or a theologian of the cross.

Before we delve into that either/or, a digression to say a word about the business of theology may be useful. We should not worry about talk of "being a theologian." We are not speaking here about being a "professional" theologian. Indeed, being a theologian of the cross has no automatic connection to what might be called "academic theology." Luther liked to say that what makes a theologian is the ability properly to distinguish between law and gospel, not ability and prowess in scholarly pursuits. Of course, it is to be hoped that the two abilities do come together in reflective Christians, especially in pastors and teachers of theology. Unfortunately, that is not always the case. But becoming a theologian of the cross is a different matter. As we shall see, it means being turned to seek out "the real" in a quite different fashion. Becoming a theologian of the cross involves turning to face the problems, joys, and sorrows of everyday life. To be sure, for some that will include being professors and academics, and the theology of the cross should affect the way they do that. It should also affect all of life in its own way. That will no doubt become clear as we look at the Heidelberg Disputation.

Suffice it to say for now, though, that all of us are theologians in one way or another. Being a theologian just means thinking and speaking about God. True, we may not do much of that. We might go for days and weeks without a thought of God entering our heads, but that is usually impossible. Things happen. Accidents. Tragedies.

Deaths and funerals. Natural disasters. Illness. Loss. Suffering. Disappointment. Wrongdoing. And so on and on. There is also good fortune. Perhaps unexpected success or escape from danger or certain disaster. Experience of great beauty or pleasure. Sheer grace. Chance encounters that determine our lives. Love. We begin to wonder. God pops into our thinking and conversation. We may cry out in agony, "Why God?" or in relief, "Thank God!" Or we may just use God's name in cursing. Sooner or later we are likely to get thinking about God and wondering if there is some logic to it all in our lives, or some injustice. We become theologians.

Becoming a theologian is not a matter to be taken lightly. We can be blessed by it if we "get it right," as well as cursed by it if we don't. Nevertheless, the task, especially for believers, is inescapable. I always remember a wise professor's warning, "Those who take up the task of theology sometimes come a-cropper, but those who refuse the task altogether will most certainly do so." With such words in mind, it should be worth our while to spend some time thinking on the logic of God and the task of becoming theologians — and what kind of theologians we ought to be. This little book is an invitation to such thinking. It invites us to the kind of thinking shaped by the cross. It is about becoming a theologian of the cross.

Returning to our either/or, it is evident that, since the two stories, the glory story and the cross story, actually determine how we think about ourselves, they quite consequently also determine what kind of theologian we are going to be. Once again we emphasize that the issue here is not the more abstract one of talking or writing *about theology* but the more difficult and concrete matter of *being theologians*. In the more famous and decisive theses of the Heidelberg Disputation (19-22) Luther does not talk about theology in the abstract but rather about the two different kinds of theologians and what they do, the way they operate. The question we have to try to deal with is what kind of theologian the two stories make out of us. The answer will be given more completely as we move through the Heidelberg Disputation. Here we only anticipate by means of a hasty sketch to alert us.

The Disputation is set up quite consistently as a series of sharp contrasts — or better, antitheses — between the two ways of being theologians and the stories that lie behind them. The antitheses focus on basic issues of salvation: the question of law and works; the power of the human will; the attempt to "see" God; the task of speaking the truth in these matters; faith; and ultimately of the love of God, which creates its own object. The argument proceeds by constantly setting the way of glory over against the way of the cross. In every instance all loopholes are closed so that the believer will in the end simply be cast on that creative love of God, which makes the object of its love out of the nothing to which the sinner has been reduced.

The Disputation itself, one might say, illustrates the manner in which theologians of the cross operate. Claimed, that is to say killed and made alive by the cross alone as *the* story, theologians of the cross attack the way of glory, the way of law, human works, and free will, because the way of glory simply operates as a defense mechanism against the cross. Theologians of glory operate with fundamentally different presuppositions about how one comes to know God. They think one can see *through* the created world and the acts of God to the invisible realm of glory beyond it, and they must think this because for the system to work there must be a "glory road," a way of law, which the fallen creature can traverse by willing and working and thus gain the necessary merit eventually to arrive at glory.

The cross too is transparent. The theologian of glory sees through the cross so as to fit it into the scheme of works. The cross "makes up" for failures along the glory road. The upshot of it all is a fundamental misreading of reality. The theologian of glory ends by calling evil good and good evil. Works are good and suffering is evil. The God who presides over this enterprise must therefore be excused from all blame for what was termed "evil." The theology of glory ends in a simplistic understanding of God. God, according to philosophers like Plato, is not the cause of all things but only what we might call "good."[11] It is hard to see how such a god could even be involved in the cross.

Theologians of the cross, however, "say what a thing is." That is, a characteristic mark of theologians of the cross is that they learn to call a spade a spade. Since the cross story alone is their story, they are not driven by the attempt to see through it, but are drawn into the story. They know that faith means to live *in* the Christ of the story. Likewise they do not believe that we come to proper knowledge of God by attempting to see through the created world to the "invisible things of God."[12] So theologians of the cross look on all things "through suffering and the cross."[13] They, in other words, are led by the cross to *look at* the trials, the sufferings, the pangs of conscience, the troubles — and joys — of daily life as God's doing and do not try to *see through* them as mere accidental problems to be solved by metaphysical adjustment. They are not driven to simplistic theodicies because with St. Paul they believe that God justifies himself precisely in the cross and resurrection of Jesus. They know that, dying to the old, the believer lives *in* Christ and looks forward to being raised with him.

Theologians of the cross therefore come to understand that the only move left is to the proclamation that issues from the story. The final task is to *do* the story to the hearers in such a way that they are incorporated into the story itself, killed and made alive by the hearing

---

11. "Then God, if he be good, is not the author of all things, as the many assert, but he is the cause of a few things only, and not of most things that occur to men. For few are the goods of human life, and many are the evils, and the good is to be attributed to God alone; of the evils the causes are to be sought elsewhere, and not in him." — Plato *Republic* 2.379.

12. Below, thesis 19.

13. Below, thesis 20.

of it. The hearers are to be claimed by the story. Thus theologians of the cross will be compelled to theologize on the story that there are no escape hatches, no loopholes. They are constrained to rule out the attempt to see through creation or the cross to some supposed secret behind it. There is no secret passage to glory. They insist that there is no other place to look but to the cross story itself. This means that a certain suspicion and polemical edge is usually evident. Theologians of the cross know the temptations of a theology of glory well and are concerned to counter them at every turn. In essence, that is what comes to expression in Luther's Heidelberg Disputation. It is a thoroughgoing exposition and refutation of a theology of glory. A passage from Luther's *Work on the Psalms* from the same period as the Heidelberg Disputation makes all this quite explicit:

> In the kingdom of his humanity and his flesh, in which we live by faith, he makes us of the same form as himself and crucifies us by making us true humans instead of unhappy and proud Gods: humans, that is, in their misery and their sin. Because in Adam we mounted up towards equality with God, he descended to be like us, to bring us back to knowledge of himself. That is the sacrament of the incarnation. That is the kingdom of faith in which the cross of Christ holds sway, which sets at naught the divinity for which we perversely strive and restores the despised weakness of the flesh which we have perversely abandoned.[14]

The passage well illustrates how the cross story becomes our story. It must not be forgotten, however, that the crucifixion is not the end of the story. The passage goes on to speak of the final hope:

> But in the kindgom of his divinity and glory he will make us like unto his glorious body, where we shall be like him and shall be

14. WA 5.128.31–5.129.4. Lenker 1:204.

no longer sinners, no longer weak, but shall ourselves be kings, the sons of God, and as the angels that are in heaven. Then we shall say "my God" in real possession, which now we say only in hope.[15]

To sum up, the two stories with the two resultant ways of being a theologian are indicative of two quite different perceptions of Christian faith and life. The theologian of glory searches endlessly for escape hatches, for a way to glory enticing enough to attract the free will (or what is left of it) of the seeker. I use the analogy of addiction throughout the book in the attempt to demonstrate the difference between the theologian of glory and the theologian of the cross. The theologian of glory is like one who considers curing addiction by optimistic exhortation. The theologian of the cross knows that the cure is much more drastic. Luther virtually invites this analogy of addiction in the proof for thesis 22 of the Disputation, when he likens the theology of glory to the thirst for money, or wisdom, or power, and so forth and declares that the soul's insatiable "thirst for glory is not ended by satisfying it but rather by extinguishing it."[16] A theologian of glory attempts

---

15. It goes without saying, perhaps, that "glory" here means something quite different from the glory in a theology of glory. The glory of God comes by God's grace and power. The glory of the theology of glory is made, sought, and appropriated by fallen creatures in the attempt to usurp divine glory.

16. LW 31.54. See the discussion below, pp. 17, 94-95. There is an enlightening treatment of the relation between sin and addiction by Linda A. Mercadante, "Sin, Addiction, and Freedom," in Rebecca S. Chopp and Mark Lewis Taylor, eds., *Reconstructing Christian Theology* (Minneapolis: Augsburg/Fortress, 1994), 220-44. Mercadante maintains that while addiction does illuminate aspects of the Christian understanding of sin, it cannot replace it. I quite agree. My use of addiction here is strictly as an analogy to illuminate differences between the operation of a theologian of glory and that of a theologian of the cross. I am quite conscious of the fact that more would have to be said to overcome some of the limitations and work out the ramifications of the analogy. For instance, it is clear from the discussion in the Heidelberg Disputation that sin as "addiction" to self can go one of two ways, addiction

to cure those addicted to glory by optimistic appeals, that is, by the law. But what happens thereby is only a reinforcement of one's illusions about oneself. The supposed optimism of the theology of glory turns against itself. When the addict discovers the impossibility of quitting, self-esteem plummets. The addict tries to hide the addiction and puts on a false front. Superficial optimism breeds ultimate despair.

A theology of glory works like that. It operates on the assumption that what we need is optimistic encouragement, some flattery, some positive thinking, some support to build our self-esteem. Theologically speaking it operates on the assumption that we are not seriously addicted to sin, and that our improvement is both necessary and possible. We need a little boost in our desire to do good works. Of course our theologian of glory may well grant that we need the help of grace. The only dispute, usually, will be about the degree of grace needed. If we are a "liberal," we will opt for less grace and tend to define it as some kind of moral persuasion or spiritual encouragement. If we are more "conservative" and speak even of the depth of human sin, we will tend to escalate the degree of grace needed to the utmost. But the hallmark of a theology of glory is that it will always consider grace as something of a supplement to whatever is left of human will and power. It will always, in the end, hold out for some free will. Theology then becomes the business of making theological explanations attractive to the will.

---

either to "baser lusts" or to higher pretensions of self-righteousness and glory. Luther uses it in this treatise in the latter sense. The "addiction" of most concern to the theologian of the cross is the attempt to bypass the cross on the strength of one's own works. The addict, likewise, may be addicted either to the substance in question or to his own obsession with quitting and become a "dry drunk." One might also ask whether the optimistic approach may not work at least in some cases. But as we shall see later, this objection will not work in the case of a theology of the cross for it is not finally doctrines about sin that convince the sinner, but precisely the cross itself. The cross makes all superficial optimism impossible.

Sooner or later a disastrous erosion of the language sets in. It must constantly be adjusted to be made appealing. Gradually it sinks to the level of maudlin sentimentality.

Theologians of the cross, however, operate quite differently. They operate on the assumption that there must be — to use the language of treatment for addicts — a "bottoming out" or an "intervention." That is to say, there is no cure for the addict on his own. In theological terms, we must come to confess that we are addicted to sin, addicted to self, whatever form that may take, pious or impious. So theologians of the cross know that we can't be helped by optimistic appeals to glory, strength, wisdom, positive thinking, and so forth because those things are themselves the problem. The truth must be spoken. To repeat Luther again, the thirst for glory or power or wisdom is never satisfied even by the acquisition of it. We always want more — precisely so that we can declare independence from God. The thirst is for the absolute independence of the self, and that is sin. Thus again Luther's statement of the radical cure in his proof for thesis 22: "The remedy for curing desire does not lie in satisfying it, but in extinguishing it."[17] The cross does the extinguishing. The cross is the death of sin, and the sinner. The cross does the "bottoming out." The cross is the "intervention." The addict/sinner is not coddled by false optimism but is put to death so that a new life can begin. The theologian of the cross "says what a thing is" (thesis 21). The theologian of the cross preaches to convict of sin. The addict is not deceived by theological marshmallows but is told the truth so that he might at last learn to confess, to say, "I am an addict," "I am an alcoholic," and never to stop saying it. Theologically and more universally all must learn to say, "I am a sinner," and likewise never to stop saying it until Christ's return makes it no longer true.

The theology of the cross is the true and ultimate source of

17. LW 31.54.

human optimism because it always presupposes the resurrection.[18] We should always bear in mind in pondering texts like the Heidelberg Disputation that resurrection is always taken together with the cross. The fundamental question of the Disputation is how to arrive at that righteousness that will enable us to stand before God. It is about resurrection, finally, even when the word is not explicitly spoken. Indeed, it is not possible to have a theology of the cross without resurrection. The powerful attacks launched against even the best of human works that put the sinner to death would simply not be possible if the resurrection were not presupposed. Some theologians of the cross seem afraid to bring in talk of resurrection because they apparently fear it will mitigate the unrelieved "tragedy" of the cross and its attack.[19] But the opposite is the case. Without the resurrection theologians will always be tempted to tone down the attack in order to leave room for at least some optimism, some hope for the survival of the old self. They end by telling sweet lies, calling the bad good and the good bad. Without the resurrection

18. James Nestingen has made the point well in his essay, "Luther's Heidelberg Disputation: An Analysis of the Argument," in *All Things New, Essays in Honor of Roy A. Harrisville*, ed. Arland J. Hultgren et al., Word and World Supplement Series, no. 1 (St. Paul: Luther Seminary, 1992), 147-48. Nestingen criticizes Jos E. Vercruysse ("Gesetz und Liebe, Die Struktur der 'Heidelberg Disputation' Luthers [1518]," *Lutherjahrbuch* 48 [1981]), to whose analysis I am indebted considerably here, for failing to see the Disputation in the light of Luther's apocalyptic view, thus missing the note of resurrection. Nestingen would like to see theses 1-18 interpreted as the cross side of the argument, and theses 19-24 as the resurrection side. That is certainly quite possible. However, I find it also important to regard the resurrection as presupposition for the entire argument. The devastating attack launched in theses 1-18 against even the best of our works, which puts the sinner to death, is simply not possible where there is no resurrection. A theology of glory is a theology premised on what Ernest Becker called "the denial of death." A theology of the cross sees that we must go through death to receive the gift of new life.

19. This is one of the questions I have about the work of Douglas John Hall, especially in its earlier stages (see, e.g., *Lighten Our Darkness*). One almost gets the impression Hall is afraid to turn to the resurrection for fear it will mitigate the unrelieved negativity of the cross vis-à-vis the "official optimism" of North America.

theologians cannot speak the truth about the human condition, and without hearing and confessing such truth we have no hope, no resurrection. For a resurrection to happen, there must first be a death. The truth must be heard and confessed; then there is hope. A new life can begin, and with it a new sense of self-worth can blossom. That is the ultimate aim of the Heidelberg Disputation. For in the end we arrive, as we shall see, at the love of God, which creates anew out of nothing. So we begin the journey.

The Heidelberg Disputation

In 1518 Luther was asked to explain and defend his "new theology" before the German Congregation of his Augustinian order in Heidelberg. As was often the case in those days, this defense took the form of theses for public debate and discussion. There are many such disputations in Luther's writings, and they are quite important because they are instances in which he "went public," so to speak, to "publicize" among theological colleagues what he considered important. Sometimes, either simultaneously or somewhat later, the theses were supplemented by paragraphs of supporting material *(probationes conclusionum)* drawn from scripture or earlier teachers of the church. In our exposition we shall here refer to them as "proofs."

Heinrich Bornkamm argues that, as far as the theology of the Reformation is concerned, the Heidelberg Disputation is the most influential of all Luther's disputations. It is theologically much more important and influential, for instance, than the Ninety-five Theses, even though the Ninety-five Theses caused more of an ecclesiastical and political stir. It is safe to say that the theological theses of the Disputation remain determinative and a center of attention even down to the present day. (We refer here to the "theological theses" because Luther also appended twelve theses from philosophy. We shall not deal with the philosophical theses here since they would draw us farther afield than we need go.) The theological influence of the Heidelberg Disputation is indicated by the fact that Luther's audience at Heidelberg included no less than six future reformers, among them leaders such as Martin Bucer and Johannes Brenz, together with other theologians who either became Luther's disciples or were decisively influenced by him.[20] Yet these pieces of public theology, with the possible exception of the Ninety-five Theses, which touched off the Reformation, remain among the least known and read of his works. No doubt that is because the theses are not easy reading. They are terse and compact, often involved with precise academic questions that are difficult to follow unless there is familiarity with some of the history and terminology behind the issues. So they need considerable exposition. Indeed it is regrettable that in spite of its importance, the Heidelberg Disputation has never received the sort of comprehensive commentary it deserves. What I attempt here can by no means pretend to be such. At best it might be considered as some reflections on the text of the Disputation. It is hoped that they will attract others to the more difficult task of a complete commentary.

Unlike many disputations of this sort, including others by Luther, the theological theses of the Heidelberg Disputation give every indication of being very carefully thought out and put together.[21] Other disputations, including even the Ninety-five Theses, give the impression of being like shots fired at random in several different directions. That does not appear to be the case with the theological theses of the Heidelberg Disputation. They are carefully

20. Heinrich Bornkamm, "Die theologischen Thesen Luthers bei der Heidelberger Disputation 1518 und seine theologia Crucis," in *Luther, Gestalt und Wirkungen*, Schriften des Vereins für Reformationsgeschichte, vol. 5, no. 188 (Gütersloher Verlagshaus Gerd Mohn, 1975), 130.

21. Bornkamm, "Die theologischen Thesen Luthers," 130. See also Vercruysse, "Gesetz und Liebe," 7.

crafted and ordered. It is not too much to say, I think, that they are almost a kind of outline for Luther's subsequent theological program. Luther called the theses "theological paradoxes." Stating the truth in the form of such paradoxes was a favorite tactic used by the reformers to attack and vex the reigning scholastic theology. Unlike Erasmus who might appeal to Origen and Jerome for more "reasonable" interpretations, Luther appealed strictly to the authority of St. Paul and his "most trustworthy interpreter" St. Augustine for his paradoxes. The aim of the Disputation and its proofs was to show that the theses were properly derived from these two authorities.

To characterize the structure of the Disputation, some interpreters have used the image of a great arch stretching between two pillars.[22] The first pillar, the law of God, is announced right off in thesis 1: "The law of God, the most salutary doctrine of life, cannot advance man on his way to righteousness, but rather hinders him." The second pillar, the love of God, is set forth in the first words of the last thesis (28): "The love of God does not find, but creates, that which is pleasing to it." So the whole Disputation moves from the question of the law of God to the love of God. The question, we might say, is how we are moved from one to the other. The theology of the cross points out how that comes about. The way from the law of God to the love of God goes through the cross.

If it is true that these theses are carefully crafted, we need to look at the structure of the Disputation more closely.[23] It can be divided into four sections. The first includes theses 1-12 and deals with the nature and worth of human works over against the question of sin. The second section (13-18) deals with the impotence of human free will to avoid sin. The third section (19-24) deals with the "great divide," the fundamental contrast between approaching

22. Bornkamm, "Die theologischen Thesen Luthers," 133.
23. Here I follow the analysis of Vercruysse, "Gesetz und Liebe."

these questions as a theologian of glory or a theologian of the cross. The fourth and final section (25-28) declares the climactic outcome of the whole movement: God's love in Christ is a creative act that brings believers into being. When all our human possibilities have been exhausted and we have been reduced to nothing, the one who creates out of nothing does his "proper work." Now we will look more closely at these sections.

THE HEIDELBERG DISPUTATION

I

The Problem of Good Works

THESES 1-12

THESIS 1. The law of God, the most salutary doctrine of life, cannot advance humans on their way to righteousness, but rather hinders them.

A most distressing paradox, and one of the hardest pills for the Old Adam and Eve to swallow! It is, however, a staple of Luther's reformation thought and practice and the first move in the attack on the theology of glory. The basic question of the Disputation is stated in this and the following thesis: What advances sinners on the way to righteousness before God? Is it the way of glory or the way of the cross? *It is imperative to recognize at the outset that since the theology of glory is under question, the whole discussion here is about the place and usefulness of* good works, *not about the perfidy of evil ones.* It is without question that evil works can't advance us toward righteousness. Even theologians of glory would agree to that premise. What then can do it? The immediate assumption of the theologian of glory is that good works done in obedience to divine law must be the way.

Hence the discussion begins with the question of the law. The insistence from the very start is that the law cannot advance us to righteousness. The law cannot save. The shocking fact is that the law is not a remedy for sin, although we never quite seem to believe that. Indeed, when righteousness before God is at stake, it only makes matters worse. So we begin with the fundamental parting of the ways, the basic distinction in stories.

Theologians are confronted at the start with basic questions about what story they are to tell. Do they tell the story of the law and merit or of the cross? Three things should be noted carefully here that sharpen the paradox. First, in this thesis it is the very law of God himself, "the most salutary doctrine of life," that is being arraigned, not some lesser or perhaps "natural" law. Second, Luther is here talking about those who stand under the revealed law of God, the people of God, not those "outside." Third, not only is this law powerless to save, but it *actually makes matters worse!* It is commonplace among evangelical Christians to believe that we can't perfectly fulfill the law, but we often try to because we assume that *if we only could* we would do it. So we believe that we must try to do something at least, and then, it is assumed, Christ will make up for our "shortcomings." But here is the bombshell: doing the law does not advance the cause of righteousness one whit. It only makes matters worse. Luther's proof for this is straightforward, from Paul and Augustine:

> This is made clear by the Apostle in his letter to the Romans (3[:21]): "But now the righteousness of God has been manifested apart from the law." St. Augustine interprets this in his book, *The Spirit and the Letter (De Spiritu et Littera):* "Without the law, that is, without its support." In Rom. 5[:20] the Apostle states, "Law intervened, to increase the trespass," and in Rom. 7[:9] he adds, "But when the commandment came, sin revived." For this reason he calls the law a law of death and a law of sin in Rom. 8[:2]. Indeed, in 2 Cor. 3[:6] he says, "the written code kills," which

St. Augustine throughout his book, *The Spirit and the Letter,* understands as applying to every law, even the holiest law of God.[1]

The question of law in Luther has always been a perplexing one. Whence comes this shockingly negative evaluation of the law? Here we see quite clearly the basis for the negative judgment and with it the gateway to any approach to the theology of the cross. It is the view straight out of Paul that righteousness before God comes "apart from the law," or with Augustine, "without its support." In other words, from the vantage point of the righteousness of faith we see that the law comes up against its absolute end. The law "finishes" its work in exposing sin and, indeed, making it worse. In terms of persistent questions about the negativity of the theology of the cross, we see here at the very outset that the theology of the cross presupposes the resurrection. Without the resurrection the absolute negation of the law as a way to glory would not be possible. The law surrenders its hold on us only when the new is given. It is only because the resurrection promises an entirely new possibility that the cross can function as absolute negation. The root of the paradox in this first thesis lies in the fact that something entirely new is afoot. The righteousness that obtains before God comes "apart from the law," through the gospel of resurrection. So we have the paradox that the very law of God does not improve sinners but makes them worse. The cross itself, we might say, is proof of that.

Perhaps we can glimpse the truth behind this paradox by recalling the analogy of addiction. The law "Thou shalt quit!" is for the alcoholic quite right and true. It is a "most salutary doctrine of life." However, it does not realize its aim but only makes matters worse. It deceives the alcoholic by arousing pride and so becomes a defense mechanism against the truth, the actuality of addiction. That is not what the law is for. Law is not intended to isolate from

1. LW 31.42-43.

God in independence and pride, but to expose the need for God and his grace. Thus the law does not cure but kills. And so it is, one way or another. It drives either to despair or to presumption. This is, of course, most offensive to us. Something in us wants to hold out till the last for the ability of the alcoholic to "get it all together" and quit. "Doesn't it work that way at least for some people?" so we cry. Perhaps this is where the analogy reaches its limits. In human affairs it may sometimes work. The addict may not be so far gone as was thought and may be able to quit. But when we shift to the relationship with God it is another matter. The "intervention," the cross itself, exposes the absolute depth and hopelessness of our addiction. Before the cross there can only be repentance. Even when the person is able to quit, he may be dancing on the edge of the abyss of pride and its constant companion, despair.

To turn from the language of the analogy back to the language of theology, it must be recognized that the righteousness we are talking about that we fail to attain through the law of God is not what was later called "civil righteousness," worldly justice, but the righteousness that enables us to stand before God. It is a sheer gift to be received only by faith, by being called into relationship as an entirely passive receiver. God, that is, insists on being related to us as the giver of the gift. What God "demands" is, as Luther will put it a bit later, "naked trust," pure receivers. To be a receiver, to believe that the gift is complete, is to be "right with God."

This means there are two ways we can miss the mark of righteousness before God, two ways the relationship can be destroyed. One is more or less obvious: outright sinfulness, unrighteousness, lawlessness, self-indulgence, what the Bible would call "worldliness" or, perhaps in more modern dress, carelessness or heedlessness. In other words, we can just say to God, "No thanks, I don't want it, I'll take my own chances." The other is much less obvious and more subtle, one that morally earnest people have much more trouble with:

turning our back on the gift and saying in effect, "I do agree with what you demand, but I don't want charity. That's too demeaning. So I prefer to do it myself. What you are offering is 'too cheap.' I prefer the law, thank you very much. That seems safer to me." What this means, of course, is that secretly we find doing it ourselves more flattering to our self-esteem — the current circumlocution for pride. The law, that is, even the law of God, "the most salutary doctrine of life," *is used as a defense against the gift.* Thus, the more we "succeed," the worse off we are. The relationship to the giver of the gift is broken. To borrow the language of addiction again, it is the addiction that destroys the relationship. The alcoholic can be either a drunk or a "dry drunk." While the latter is socially preferable, there is little to choose between them in a broader religious view. One can be addicted either to what is base or to what is high, either to lawlessness or to lawfulness. Theologically there is not any difference since both break the relationship to God, the giver.

Therefore the law can't save us. To think that it can is the fundamental mistake of the theologian of glory. The law is not a remedy for sin. It does not cure sin but rather makes it worse. St. Paul says it was given to make sin apparent, indeed, even to *increase* it. It doesn't do that necessarily by increasing immorality, although that can happen when rebellion or the power of suggestion leads us to do just what the law is against. But what the theologian of the cross sees clearly from the start is that, more perversely, the law multiplies sin precisely through our morality, our misuse of the law and our success at it. It becomes a defense against the gift. That is the very essence of sin: refusing the gift and thereby setting the self in place of God.

Thus there is a mighty offense right away in this first thesis. There is something in us that is always suspicious of or rebels against the gift. The defense that it is too cheap, easy, or morally dangerous is already the protest of the Old Adam and Eve who fear — rightly! — that their house is under radical attack. Since they are entrenched behind the very law of God as their last and most pious defense, the attack must indeed be radical. It is a battle to the death. It won't be cheap. Those so addicted to self that they misuse the law of God as a defense against God will not likely be improved by better instruction or pious optimism. Current religiosity and ethics, especially those that replace the story of the cross with demands for social reform, have produced many a theology of glory. It still flourishes along with its attendant despair. There is no cure through the law. It will take some dying. So we are already on the way to the cross.

> THESIS 2. Much less can human works, which are done over and over again with the aid of natural precepts, so to speak, lead to that end.

This thesis extends the focus of the first thesis to include not only works done under the revealed law of God but also those done according to the constant prompting of "natural powers" within. Its point is that if the revealed law of God cannot advance fallen beings toward righteousness, natural powers under the prodding of the moral law within are much less able to do so. Theses 1 and 2 thus mirror Paul's argument in Romans 2 and 3 about the failure of both Jews under the revealed law and Gentiles who show that they have the law written in their hearts. Both are under indictment and have gone astray. The proof says it quite plainly:

> Since the law of God, which is holy and unstained, true, just, etc., is given [to] man by God as an aid beyond his natural powers to enlighten him and move him to do the good, and nevertheless the opposite takes place, namely, that he becomes more wicked, how can he, left to his own power and without such aid, be induced to do good? If a person does not do good with help from

without, he will do even less by his own strength. Therefore the Apostle, in Rom. 3[:10-12], calls all persons corrupt and impotent who neither understand nor seek God, for all, he says, have gone astray.[2]

Luther's argument here reflects a long-standing debate within theology about whether we must or can do something by our natural powers to prepare for or advance in grace. Everyone agreed, of course, that it was impossible to be saved without grace. The question, however, was whether we could or should do something, at least, to prepare for grace. Luther rejected such claims out of hand. They will come up again in theses 13 and following regarding the question of free will.

We should perhaps note, however, that the issues reflected here are not just ancient history. The modern world too tends to reject the law of God as a word from without. The self is encouraged to turn inward to the "moral law within" and the self's own inner resources for assurance and power. Whatever may be the usefulness of such encouragement in the human sphere, this thesis insists that it can hardly advance the cause of righteousness before God. If the most holy law of God, given from without to enlighten, inspire, and move, only makes humans worse, how can turning inward upon ourselves be of any help? The cross makes it clear that the law, whether from without or within, is a dead-end street when it comes to the question of righteousness before God. For the law demands love. It is quite right in so doing. It is "holy, just, and good." But it is not able to produce or induce what it demands. Law is over when the gift of love comes. In Leif Grane's fine phrase, "What the law requires is freedom from the law!"[3] Or as Luther could say,

---

2. LW 31.43.

3. Leif Grane, *The Augsburg Confession: A Commentary*, translated by John H. Rasmussen (Minneapolis: Augsburg, 1987), 67-68.

putting words in God's mouth, "I am obliged to forgive them their sins if I want the law fulfilled by them; indeed, I must also put away the law, for I see that they are unable not to sin, especially when they are fighting, that is, when they are laboring to fulfill the law in their own."[4] What God finally wants is for us to do what the law points to but can't accomplish: the freedom, joy, and spontaneity of faith, hope, and love. But that is, of course, an entirely different story!

> THESIS 3. Although the works of man always seem attractive and good, they are nevertheless likely to be mortal sins.
>
> THESIS 4. Although the works of God are always unattractive and appear evil, they are nevertheless really eternal merits.

Theses 3 and 4 begin an extended discussion of human works in contrast to divine works. In so doing they set forth right at the beginning the basis for the fundamental difference between one who thinks and acts as a theologian of glory and one who thinks and acts as a theologian of the cross. As we have already set forth in our introduction, there are two fundamentally different stories, two different bases for faith. Indeed, we can say there are two fundamentally different types of "religion." To use our analogy, there is the religion based on optimistic appeals to the addict's internal resources and that based on the recognition of the need for an "intervention" from without. Theologically that translates into a faith based on human works and one based on the works of God. The statements about "the works of God" here begin the introduc-

4. LW 33.218.

tion of the new story. But it is not easy to see. We are too blinded by the glory of human works. So we must note in these theses the concern for the problem of appearance and seeing.

Theses 3 and 4 can be taken together because they are parallel in construction and set up the fundamental contrast. These theses are basic for Luther's entire theology and already anticipate theses 19-22, particularly thesis 21, which maintains that the theologian of glory calls evil good and good evil. Even more, theses 3 and 4 sound the note of "contraries" that runs through all of Luther's theology. Since we are inveterate theologians of glory, God cannot come appealing to our religious aspirations. Therefore God's revelation can take place only under the form of opposites, *sub contrario*. God does his alien and wrathful work before he does his proper and loving work; he makes alive by killing, brings to heaven by going through hell, brings forth mercy out of wrath.

Consequently, these theses are indispensable for the theologian of the cross. They set forth what has to guide the language of the theologians of the cross if they are to speak the truth about human and divine works, to "say what a thing is." Each member of one thesis finds its contrary in the other. Furthermore, within each thesis there is a further contrast between appearance and reality. The contraries can be set up as follows:[5]

3. The Works of Humans	4. The Works of God
Always look splendid	Always look deformed
Appear to be good	Appear to be bad
Are nevertheless in all probability	Are nevertheless in very truth
Mortal sins	Immortal merits

As the two theses arranged in contrasting columns bear out, human works are here set in diametric opposition to the works

5. Translated and adapted from Vercruysse, "Gesetz und Liebe," 11-12.

of God. But within each column there is a further opposition between appearance and reality. The theologian of glory is bound of necessity to put a false evaluation on human works. There is literally nowhere else to turn. As was developed in the first two theses, the theologian of glory is compelled to use the works of the law as a defense against the sheer gift of God. Therefore things are not what they seem. The works look good and, indeed, give every appearance of being good. In reality, however, precisely because of the goodness attributed to them and consequently the trust invested in them, they are in all probability deadly sins. The point of the argument is that estimating the value of our works is by no means just a neutral enterprise. It is, of course, highly offensive to have the best of our works under the law judged to be deadly sins. The proof of the thesis, however, comes from Jesus' words in Matthew 23:27, which speaks about this difference between appearance and reality:

> Woe to you, scribes and Pharisees, hypocrites! for you are like whitewashed tombs, which on the outside look beautiful, but inside they are full of the bones of the dead and of all kinds of filth. So you also on the outside look righteous to others, but inside you are full of hypocrisy and lawlessness.

Perhaps the most telling proof that works done in human strength are really deadly sins comes again from St. Paul in Galatians 3:10, "All who rely on the works of the law are under the curse." Since human works outside of grace are works of the law, they stand under the curse. Therefore they are deadly sins, not just venial ones.[6]

---

6. Luther is here alluding to the distinction between mortal and venial sins used in medieval penitential practice. A mortal sin is generally regarded as a transgression of God's law of such seriousness that it causes loss of the effects of grace, rendering the sinner subject to eternal punishment. It can involve excommunication. A venial sin is a more minor error and does not entail loss of grace. However, it

The proof for thesis 4 is a little compendium of passages much beloved by Luther, setting forth his understanding of God's work "under the form of opposites" over against human works. Isaiah 53 quite naturally heads the list:

> That the works of God are unattractive is clear from what is said in Isa. 53[:2], "He had no form or comeliness," and in 1 Sam. 2[:6] "The Lord kills and brings to life; he brings down to Sheol and raises up." This is understood to mean that the Lord humbles and frightens us by means of the law and the sight of our sins so that we seem in the eyes of men, as in our own, as nothing, foolish, and wicked, for we are in truth that. Insofar as we acknowledge and confess this, there is no form or beauty in us, but our life is hidden in God (i.e., in the bare confidence in his mercy), finding in ourselves nothing but sin, foolishness, death, and hell, according to that verse of the Apostle in 2 Cor. 6[:9-10] "As sorrowful, yet always rejoicing; as dying and behold we live." And that it is which Isa. 28[:2] calls the alien work of God that he may do his work (that is, he humbles us thoroughly, making us despair, so that he may exalt us in his mercy, giving us hope), just as Hab.

---

does require some submission to penitential discipline. We will encounter this distinction again later.

I prefer here to use the less loaded term "deadly sin" to convey what Luther seems to have in mind. He is already in the process of moving away from the traditional distinction between mortal and venial sin — a slippery distinction to work with in any case! For Luther in this disputation, I believe, a "deadly sin" is not merely an obvious violation of law — a crime, for instance — that all, even the sinner, would likely condemn and confess. A deadly sin is more likely a work whose apparent goodness is such that it seduces us into trusting in it and our own doing of it. They are works, as thesis 3 puts it, that appear good. They lead, therefore, to an actual despising of the very unconditionality of the grace of God. In that real sense they actually do cut one off from grace. The symptoms of such deadly sin are present when grace is ridiculed for being "too cheap," or when permissiveness, moral laxity, and so forth are present. The assumption is that grace is not enough and needs the addition of what is here called "human works."

3[:2] states, "In wrath remember mercy." Such a man therefore is displeased with all his works; he sees no beauty, but only his depravity. Indeed, he also does those things that appear foolish and disgusting to others.

This depravity, however, comes into being in us either when God punishes us or when we accuse ourselves, as 1 Cor. 11[:31] says, "If we judged ourselves truly, we should not be judged" by the Lord. Deut. 32[:36] also states, "The Lord will vindicate his people and have compassion on his servants." In this way, consequently, the unattractive works that God does in us, that is, those that are humble and devout, are really eternal, for humility and fear of God are our entire merit.[7]

A radical reversal in our seeing takes place when we encounter the one who "had no form or comeliness that we should desire him," the one from whom we "hid our faces," who "was despised and we esteemed him not." Especially to be noted in this proof are the many instances that have to do with seeing or not seeing, appearance and reality, discovering, acknowledging, finding, and making accurate judgments about ourselves. There is a fundamental difference in the way reality is perceived. The theologian of glory judges by appearances and so classifies works as good or bad. But that really means that such theologians *see through* the works to an eternal standard by which they are evaluated. Everyone will no doubt admit that the works are not perfect. Nevertheless, it will be insisted that there is, as the saying goes, "good in them." As such they are taken to be more or less pale or defective copies of the transcendent perfect good and so can be trusted as meritorious — at least in a limited sense. This means that what is bad or unattractive in them is disregarded. It is not to be credited to God's account. Evil, to this way of looking at the matter, is "non-being." The intellect, Luther

7. LW 31.44

will say later, simply cannot see it.[8] This is what it means to say
that the theologian of glory does not look at it but "sees through
it." Thus the works remain all the while "human works" no matter
how much they are assisted by "grace." Whatever good there is must
be credited to the human account.

Theologians of the cross, however, cannot see through the
"unattractive" and apparently evil works of God. They cannot see
through such works because they have been "gotten at" by suffering
and the cross (thesis 20, below). They see God working exactly
through the horror of the cross. God's hidden and alien working in
the cross is such that it reflects back on us and exposes our own
lives. Thus the works do not become the occasion for pride, but
rather humility and despair. We are led therefore not to credit our
own account but to judge ourselves and to confess. The human
works that once seemed attractive and good now have no form or
beauty and are the cause of sorrow and despair. If we see clearly, if
we are able to "say what a thing is," we should be able to judge
ourselves so that we do not come under the judgment of God.

It is of utmost importance to see here that what Luther is
talking about is quite actual, even down to the present day. The
most consistent complaint about being a theologian of the cross
is that one sets forth a view of life that is much too negative,
gloomy, and depressing. But that is simply to repeat in contemporary jargon what Luther has been saying: "The works of God
are always unattractive and appear evil. . . ." Our complaint —
as is generally true of arguments with Luther! — does not really
refute the argument but rather just illustrates it. We actually do
"hide our faces" and look for something more "positive, self-
affirming, and attractive." And so we don't see. We can't look. We

8. Luther mentions the relationship between failure of sight and nonbeing in
the final sentences of the proof for the last thesis (28) of the Disputation. One wishes
he had made more of it!

call evil good and good evil. As addicts, as theologians of glory, we have no choice.

So it is quite apparent that being able to see is not something we can accomplish. The light shines in a very dark place indeed![9] The last sentence in the proof makes clear that the "works of God" Luther has in mind are those that *God works in us* through the one who was despised and rejected so that we might begin to see the way things are. It is what we see when we look at the world "through suffering and the cross" (thesis 20). The works of God in us, the humility and fear of God, are our "eternal merit." Our lives are hidden in God, Luther says, and he explains that by saying that we live only in "naked confidence in the mercy of God."[10] So to live is not gloomy or depressing, but rather "As sorrowful, yet always rejoicing; as dying, and behold we live" (2 Cor. 6:9-10).

THESIS 5. The works of men are thus not mortal sins (we speak of works that are apparently good), as though they were crimes.

THESIS 6. The works of God (we speak of those that he does through man) are thus not merits, as though they were sinless.

Again we find parallel and contrasting assertions. The purpose here is to pinpoint and bring the sinfulness of humans more clearly to light by the light of the cross. The focus is on good works — those on the one hand that humans do in their own power (thesis 5) and those on the other hand that God does in us and through them. To say that

9. LW 31.52. See below, chap. 3, n. 14.
10. LW 31.44.

those human works which appear to be good are nevertheless deadly sins (thesis 3) does not mean that they are criminal acts of the sort that society in general would certainly call evil. On the contrary, they are acts that appear morally good and beneficial. Such apparently good works are nevertheless deadly sins, because they are *human* works, and are thus bad fruit from a bad tree.

Luther here points to a deepening of the concept of mortal or deadly sin. What makes a sin "mortal" or "deadly"? Not just that it is a violation of law so flagrant that everyone would condemn it. We would quite readily recognize and perhaps even confess to that. A deadly sin is one that actually separates and seals us off from God. That occurs when the apparent goodness of our works seduces us into putting our trust in them, that is, it occurs when the very goodness of the work is such that it dissuades us from confessing. We are in reality then, not just in theory, sealed off from grace. As we put it earlier, the works of the law are used as a defense against the very unconditionality of the gift of grace. A human work, no matter how good, is deadly sin because it in actual fact entices us away from "naked trust in the mercy of God" to a trust in self. The symptoms of such deadly sin can be detected, therefore, in the very midst of our piety when complaint is unthinkingly launched against the "cheapness" of grace, or the fear that it leads too readily to moral laxity, permissiveness, and so forth. These are words that bespeak trust in the apparent goodness of human works and distrust in the power of divine grace. Thus they cut the sinner off from God — deadly sin! In actual fact we fall very easily into calling evil good and good evil!

This means, consequently, that we must be very careful about how we regard even those works God does in us. Deadly sin lurks in the most pious places. This is the concern of thesis 6. Even those works that God does in us are not accounted as "eternal merits" because they are supposedly sinless. None of our works, not even those done in us by God, are sinless. Luther's proof is a discussion of Ecclesiastes 7:20, "Surely there is not a righteous man on earth who does good and never sins." Some would want to interpret the passage to say that a righteous man may indeed sin, but not when he is doing good. Luther dismisses that interpretation by claiming that had the Holy Spirit meant that it would have been said much simpler: "There is not a righteous man on earth who does not sin." But it is not the habit of the Holy Spirit to babble such platitudes. The passage should be taken to mean therefore that even the good deeds done in the righteous by God are not sinless. That is to say, the righteous are simultaneously just and sinners *(simul iustus et peccator)*, a fundamental tenet of Luther's doctrine of sin and grace. Being theologians of the cross means also looking at *ourselves* through suffering and the cross and being able to "say what a thing is," to confess the truth. We look to God and not to ourselves — not even to those works that God does in us.

THESIS 7. The works of the righteous would be mortal sins if they would not be feared as mortal sins by the righteous themselves out of pious fear of God.

What then makes the difference? When is a good work a deadly sin and when not? Thesis 7 introduces a new note that is determinative for the rest of the discussion of works through thesis 12. It is the issue of the fear of God. We cannot understand the radicalness of this thesis unless we note carefully that the concern here is not for mere human works, works done by pure natural power alone. That is the concern of the next thesis. Here the focus is precisely the works *of the righteous,* those works done, it is to be assumed, with the very aid of grace. The radical claim is that the works even of the righteous are deadly sins when there is no fear of God. The tradition was willing to grant that the works of the righteous could be sinful in some way, but not deadly (mortal). So a distinction was made between venial and mortal sin. The works of the righteous could no doubt be venial but not mortal sins. Venial sins traditionally were "excusable" and did not sever the sinner from grace and the church. Submission to penitential discipline was prescribed to "make amends" but not to restore one to grace. Mortal sins were a more serious matter. Originally mortal sins were considered unforgivable (idolatry/apostasy, murder, adultery). Some confusion was introduced when the church later moved to grant forgiveness even for mortal sins upon proper repentance and penance. Mortal sins, it seems, were more serious in that they cut the sinner off from grace and can entail excommunication. More explicit acts of repentance and penance are required to restore one to the offices of grace.

Luther undercuts this very convenient distinction by introducing the question of the fear of God. If the righteous are to do their works, either bad or good, it seems, in the supposed confidence that they are at worst only venial sins, they are presuming on and usurping the judgment of God. In acting thus without genuine fear of God, their works, no matter how good, are deadly (mortal) sins. When then are the works of the righteous not mortal sins? When they fear that they are! Fear of God is the decisive issue. It should lead especially the righteous to fear that even their good deeds are deadly sins. The apparent goodness of the deed, and even the claim of the help of grace, does not remove the possibility that the act is a deadly sin. Everything depends on whether it is done in the fear of God. All this follows, Luther maintains, from what has already been said in thesis 4, where the final sentence of the proof maintains that humility and fear of God — those "unattractive" works of God in us — are our "eternal merit":

> To trust in works, which one ought to do in fear, is equivalent to giving oneself the honor and taking it from God, to whom fear is due in connection with every work. But this is completely

wrong, namely to please oneself, to enjoy oneself in one's own works, and to adore oneself as an idol. He who is self-confident and without fear of God, however, acts entirely in this manner. For if he had fear he would not be self-confident, and for this reason he would not be pleased with himself, but he would be pleased with God.[11]

Once again we come up hard against things that "are always unattractive and appear evil." The fear of God was not a popular item in Luther's day just as it is not on today's theological menu. We hardly know what to do with the repeated admonition in Luther's *Small Catechism* that we should "fear and love God." Indeed, we are big on love. That God is love and that we ought to love him in return are the repeated refrains of almost every Sunday School lesson and weekly sermon. But what of the fear of God? In order to promote a sentimentalized love we try to excuse God from everything that might cause us to fear him. Or we try to handle the matter therapeutically, making distinctions that turn us inward to examine our subjective attitudes. The fear of God being admonished by Luther, we are told, is not "servile" fear, that is, the terror of a servant expecting punishment for doing a bad job. Thus we assure ourselves that it is not a being frightened or scared by God but rather a "filial" fear, the fear that a child may have of disappointing a loving parent. It is just a falling short, perhaps, of the expectations of a love that nevertheless remains constant. But such reassurances usually only make matters worse. They turn us inward and force us to wonder what kind of fear we have — if any.

Later in the Reformation movement there was serious argument about whether true repentance was produced by fear of punishment under the law or "genuine" fear of God under the

11. LW 31.46.

gospel. Luther refused to invest much concern in such arguments when they focused on the internal churnings of the psyche: "A person in the midst of such terrors," he said, "can rarely distinguish the motivation."[12] How are we to know what kind of fear we have? Or how are we to produce the proper sort? The questions only make matters worse. We would have to fear that we did not have the proper sort of fear! What sort of fear gripped Isaiah when he saw the Lord high and lifted up among the six-winged seraphim and cried out, "Woe is me for I am a man of unclean lips . . . ," or Moses when he heard the Lord out of the burning bush, or Peter when he begged the Lord to depart from him, a sinful man, after the miraculous draft of fishes? Was it a rather mild filial fear? Or even just fear of punishment? We hardly get that impression from the narrative! Luther knew there was no way to limit, circumscribe, adequately describe, or even prescribe this fear. Perhaps it is safest just to say that it is the overwhelming sense of awe and, yes, no doubt even terror upon falling into the hands of the living God, something more like the "mystery tremendous" (*mysterium tremendum:* more literally, perhaps, a mystery that causes awe and trembling) that Rudolph Otto spoke of.[13] It will likely have many dimensions.

12. See the essay by Timothy Wengert, "Fear and Love in the Ten Commandments," *Concordia Journal* 21.1 (1995): 23. Wengert quotes from Luther's letter to Melanchthon: "How the fear of punishment and fear of God differ is more easily said with syllables and letters than known in reality and feeling" (WA Briefe 4.272.16-17). The argument in question was the first Antinomian controversy in which Agricola and Melanchthon were chief protagonists. Agricola claimed in opposition to Melanchthon that true repentance and sorrow for sin did not arise from fear of punishment, but rather from the fear of God worked by the gospel and faith. Melanchthon had insisted in the Saxon Visitation Articles that faith in the gospel was always to be preceded by preaching the law with such vigor that one would be terrified by the prospect of God's punishment.

13. Rudolph Otto, *The Idea of the Holy: An Inquiry into the Non-rational Factor in the Idea of the Divine and Its Relation to the Rational,* 2nd ed. (New York: Oxford University Press, 1950).

The point here is that when we have no fear of the Lord and we instead presume to come before the Lord bustling with self-confidence in our own accomplishments, enjoying ourselves in our works, as Luther puts it, our works are deadly sins even if we think they are done with the help of grace. For then our works stand between us and God; they usurp the honor belonging only to God. This is a transgression of the first commandment. The self sets itself as an idol. Piety is no protection.

Fear of God on the contrary means precisely letting God be God. True, the fear of God is something of a stranger in the contemporary house of religious experience with its saccharine love-piety. But perhaps there are hints and remnants of what such fear means in the argument before us. As theologians of glory we react against the idea that our best works may be deadly sins. Why? Is it out of fear? Fear that we are reduced to nothing before God? Fear that the sovereign mercy of God is an attack we as old beings cannot survive? Could that be what the Psalmist had in mind when he cried "out of the depths": "If thou, O Lord, shouldst mark iniquities, Lord, who could stand? But there is forgiveness with thee, *that thou mayest be feared*" (Ps. 130:3-4)? Perhaps the unconditional mercy of God is the only place left now where a spark of the fear of God is kindled! It strikes at least antipathy and maybe even an echo of terror into the heart of the self-assured.

The remaining paragraphs of the proof for thesis 7 are concerned with solidifying the claim that even the righteous are sinners whose works are, without the fear of God, not just venial but deadly sins. As pointed out above, the scholastic tradition generally held that, since the sins of the righteous were venial but not deadly (mortal), they did not stand in need of confession and repentance. To trouble such self-assurance, Luther cites several scriptural passages containing cries of confession and repentance from the righteous: Psalm 143:2, "Enter not into judgment with thy servant"; Psalm 32:5, "I said, 'I will confess my transgressions unto the

Lord'"; the Lord's prayer, "Forgive us our trespasses . . ."; and Revelation 21:27, "Nothing unclean shall enter into [the Kingdom of heaven]," that is, not even the righteous with their "venial" sins. For Luther such prayers of the righteous clearly indicate that they considered themselves as standing in fear of God, constantly in need of repentance and forgiveness, without which they would be lost. Thus the distinction between mortal and venial sins is effectively undercut. What matters is not the degree of the sin but whether there is true fear of God. This is true even, indeed one should say *especially,* for the righteous.

> **THESIS 8.** By so much more are the works of man mortal sins when they are done without fear and in unadulterated, evil self-security.

Thesis 8 simply continues the contrapuntal comparison of the works of the righteous versus "human works," that is, works done by and in the pure confidence of "natural power" alone. If the works even of the righteous are not just venial but deadly sins when done without fear of God, quite obviously works done entirely without fear of God in complete self-security or heedlessness are all the more deadly. All of this, Luther says in the proof, follows quite naturally from the previous thesis: "For where there is no fear there is no humility. Where there is no humility there is pride, and where there is pride there are the wrath and judgment of God, for God opposes the haughty. Indeed, if pride would cease there would be no sin anywhere."[14]

14. LW 31.47.

THESIS 9. To say that works without Christ are dead, but not mortal, appears to constitute a perilous surrender of the fear of God.

THESIS 10. Indeed, it is very difficult to see how a work can be dead and at the same time not a harmful and mortal sin.

Theses 9 and 10 belong together and undercut another scholastic distinction that compromises the true fear of God, the distinction between dead works and deadly (mortal) works. Theses 7 and 8 have insisted that works done without fear of God by either the righteous or unrighteous are mortal sins. But theologians of glory are always looking for loopholes. What is one to say of works that are genuinely good but done by nonbelievers, that is, works "without Christ"? Are they also simply mortal sins? It is a question any theology professor knows well. Students constantly worry about the "benevolent pagan." The scholastic tradition tried to handle this, as usual, by making a distinction between works that are *dead* but not *deadly* (mortal). Good works done "without Christ" are said to be dead in the sense that (being without grace) they are not meritorious, but still they were not such as to be mortal, that is, deserving of eternal condemnation. There was apparently some debate over whether the works actually prepared one for grace or even earned some lesser punishment.

Luther finds the distinction both perilous for piety and ultimately incomprehensible. Once again the issue is the fear of God. To say that a work is dead but not deadly is perilous for piety because it leaves the unbeliever some room for avoiding the crisis inherent in the command to fear God. As long as we can comfort ourselves that our works are only dead, but not deadly, we can "postpone" both giving glory to God and, consequently, turning to God. Thus, for Luther the scholastic distinction between dead and deadly is a very dangerous move that will only result in taking glory from God and delaying the conversion of the unbeliever. We do the unbeliever no favors thereby. "For if that person offends [God] who withdraws glory from him, how much more does that person offend him who continues to withdraw glory from him and does this boldly!"[15] Theological attempts to be "gracious" to the nonbeliever only lead to further disaster.

In addition, as thesis 11 points out, the distinction is well-nigh incomprehensible. How can a work be dead and at the same time not be deadly? Neither scripture nor ordinary grammar make such a confusing distinction. In common speech "dead" is worse than "deadly." A dead work is one that has no life at all, whereas a deadly or mortal work at least has the power to kill. In scripture God despises "dead" works — as when he counts the sacrifices of the wicked to be an abomination (Prov. 15:8). The distinction only leads us to favor that which God abominates.

Luther concludes by pointing out the confusion that results for the will by making such a distinction. What is the attitude of the will toward "dead" works? Approval or disapproval, love or hate? A "good" will ought, of course, to disapprove and hate works that are dead. However, it cannot since it is fallen and evil. Since it can't be neutral, the will of the sinner is bound to favor its own works. Thus it will end by loving dead works in defiance of the God it is obligated to love and honor in all things. The will is drawn into loving what is dead. But this is monstrous. If it were simply said forthrightly that works without Christ are deadly before God, there would be no such confusion.

This may seem an abstract and academic point, but once again a moment's honesty — saying what a thing is — will reveal its actuality. In fact, we do find ourselves bound to love what is here called "dead works." That is the source of the constant pressure about the

15. LW 31.47.

merit of "good works" done by unbelievers. We want so piously to do them the favor of according merit to their works. It is of course true that there is a place for such works. Later Luther would place them under the auspices of God's "left hand rule," or speak of them as "civil righteousness." But that is not to say they are dead; it is rather to grant them a kind of goodness, though limited to this age. The point here is about the spiritual peril, impropriety, and confusion of will that results from trying to create a place for such works by claiming they are dead but not deadly. Instead of honestly saying they are good, in the sense of civil righteousness, they are called dead. So once again, to save the system the theologian of glory ends in the curious position of calling the bad good and the good bad at the same time. Good works without Christ are called bad (dead) and yet good in the sense that they are not deadly (mortal) and may even lessen eternal punishment.

> **THESIS 11.** Arrogance cannot be avoided or true hope be present unless the judgment of condemnation is feared in every work.

> **THESIS 12.** In the sight of God sins are then truly venial when they are feared by men to be mortal.

Theses 11 and 12 conclude the investigation of divine versus human work. They speak of the only stance appropriate for the God-fearing believer given the development in theses 1-10. The question with which the disputation began was, What advances the sinner on the way to righteousness? The utter futility of human work in contributing anything toward this advance has now been relentlessly exposed. To repeat what was said at the outset, it must not escape attention that the focus throughout has been on *good* works, not on evil ones.

Every loophole is closed. Humans must confess not only that their best works are sinful, but also that in the very fact that they resist such judgment and pride themselves in their works, their works are actually deadly (mortal) sin. All the pious escape routes are sealed: the holiness of divine law; the goodness of works done by natural powers; the merit of works done by the righteous; the distinction between dead and deadly works — all are exposed as perilous diversions from true fear of God.

What then is the appropriate stance for the God-fearing believer? This is the burden of theses 11 and 12. Is it really possible even for believers to live as Luther has suggested, in naked trust in the mercy of God, rejecting all creaturely support and the consolation of one's "works"? Luther answers the question in the proof for thesis 11:

> It is impossible to trust in God unless one has despaired in all creatures and knows that nothing can profit one without God. Since there is no person who has this pure hope, as we said above, and since we still place some confidence in the creature, it is clear that we must, because of impurity in all things, fear the judgment of God. Thus arrogance must be avoided, not only in the work but in the inclination also, that is, it must displease us still to have confidence in the creature.[16]

Luther knows that due to sin it is impossible to avoid creaturely confidence completely. Arrogance always attends the slightest success. To avoid it not only in works but also in affections we must fear the judgment of God in every work. Thesis 12 gives some indication of the shape of this judgment. When are sins truly venial (i.e., forgivable)? When they are feared to be mortal! Luther here employs the distinction between venial and mortal sin in its original

16. LW 31.48.

sense to undercut its use. Sins are truly forgivable when they are feared to be damning. All possibility of confidence in our own works and all pleading on the basis of the distinction are impossible. This, of course, seems quite depressing to inveterate theologians of glory. Yet we should not miss the new note that sounds out of the rubble of rejected human works. It is the note of hope. It is not possible, Luther declares, for *true hope* to be present unless the judgment of condemnation is feared in every work. Every hope built on human work will prove untrue. The hope that arises out of the ashes of the refining fire will not disappoint. The way, however, is the way of the cross.

II

The Problem of Will

THESES 13-18

Thesis 13 begins the discussion of a different aspect of the problem. The question at the outset, the reader will recall, was how humans can advance on the path to righteousness. Theses 1 through 12 deal with the question of our objective deeds. The theologian of glory seeks by hook or by crook to find a place for such deeds in the cause of our righteousness before God. But the idea that such deeds, no matter how good, with or without the aid of Christ, could advance us on the path to righteousness is rejected from every angle. In theses 13-18 Luther turns to the subjective side of the question, the question of will. Can or does the will help to advance the cause? Do we actually will, that is, *want*, the righteousness that avails before God? Virtually all of Western Christendom, following St. Augustine, was agreed that without the aid of grace the will is bound and can do nothing to merit salvation. But what do such assertions mean? Must we not, do we not, make our decision for Christ when all is said and done? The theological problem arises out of the recognition and confession that we are saved by grace *alone*. If we are overwhelmed and captivated by grace *alone*, can we claim to play a part in the matter? Yet the specter of force always rears its ugly head. So to defend themselves, theologians of glory are always driven to claim

49

at least some freedom of choice and to play theological games, bargaining for little bits. In one way or another the claim is made that the will must have at least a small part to play.

In Luther's day, the argument was reduced to whether the will could — and should — at least be involved in *preparing* for the reception of grace. It was generally conceded that without grace the will could do nothing to merit eternal salvation. So it could be said that we are saved only by grace. However, the question was whether or not the will must at least desire and prepare for grace. Looming in the background always is the troublesome question of predestination. Unless we are to say that grace is given — even forcibly — here and there only to those secretly predestined, must not our wills have something to do with it? Must we not at least will to receive grace and do the best we can to get it? How can we be sure that we have received it if it is some mysterious something decided upon in eternity and not relative to human willing? Is there no way that we can discover the logic of the system? Luther's teachers were from a particular branch of late medieval scholasticism (Nominalism) that held that if we "do what is in us," that is, if we do our best, we can be assured that God will not fail to give us the desired grace.[1] So we always come back to the question of the "little bit," one of the telltale signs of the theology of glory. This is the issue in theses 13-18. Can we or will we by our own natural powers, doing our best, prepare for the reception of grace? Are we free to will that? Does the will actually want to receive grace?

The question of will and its freedom over against God and his

---

1. The well-known Latin phrase is *facere quod in se est*, "do what is in you." In modern parlance it might aptly be translated "just do your best" or "do what you can," and God will not deny you grace. The actual phrase appears in theses 13 and 16. It is intended to give comfort and assurance: What more can one do than one's best? But of course it only makes matters worse. For then the question becomes, "When can I be sure I have done my best?" One always goes out of the frying pan and into the fire by such moves.

sovereign grace has, of course, always been a difficult one for biblical faith. When it is asserted that we are saved by divine election, the protest is always raised, "We aren't puppets, are we? If everything happens by divine will, how can we be held responsible? We just can't accept such a God! There *must* be some freedom of choice!" But the point is that this kind of protest is precisely the proof of the pudding. It is evidence of theologians of glory at work defending themselves to the end. They actually admit that they cannot and will not "will" God to be God. Theologians of the cross who "see what a thing is" perceive what is going on here. They see finally that the will is bound to itself and cannot will God. This is just an honest observation of the truth of the matter, seeing the way things are. The will cannot move. It must say no to God, it wills so to do, and so will do it. If there is to be salvation, it cannot come by the will's own movement. That means there must be a death and a resurrection. The cross stands behind the question of the will. The cross itself is the evidence that we did not choose him but that he, nevertheless, chose us (John 15:16).

It is well to remember that Luther's interest here lies primarily in the area of our relationship as fallen beings to God in all his majesty. We cannot here even begin to enter that vast labyrinth! Suffice it to say that later in Luther's argument with Erasmus he will make a distinction that is helpful in keeping matters in focus. He says that if we are to use the term "free will" at all, we should limit it to our everyday freedom in those things that are below us but not attempt to extend it to those things that are "above us."[2] What does that mean? It is simply, once again, an attempt to give account of the way things are. In our daily life and affairs we do relatively what we please and God does not noticeably interfere, whatever we may believe about him. We come and go as we will;

---

2. LW 33.70. For a fuller discussion of the issue see my *Theology Is for Proclamation* (Minneapolis: Fortress, 1990), 39-56.

we decide what to wear, what to eat, what to do or not do, and so on. We may even decide to be moral or religious. We may even decide that Jesus is a wonderful person and a stirring example, and so forth. We may, supposedly, even decide whether or not to go to church. All of that is "below" us. This is Luther's way of recognizing that we actually do exercise what we call free choice in such matters. That is just the way things are. It also indicates that Luther has no particular interest or concern about what philosophers call "determinism" because in actuality it makes no difference. We go ahead and do what we please in any case, whatever we may hold philosophically.

When we come up against God, however, the living one who is really and truly *above* us, we encounter a fundamentally different problem. Luther is concerned about how we actually react to God. The problem is that we can't stand the idea of someone actually *above* us. We can't accept an electing God. We will not will it. Thus, regarding that which is truly above us, the will is not free but bound. Not forced — no one forces us to say no — we are just bound to do it! Then we begin to see into the depths of fallenness. We do not want the God of grace alone. It would be safer, we think (the ultimate blasphemy!), if we made the decision ourselves — at least just a little bit! So we come to the theses on the power of the will. They are concerned with how the will relates to that which is above us.

THESIS 13. Free will, after the fall, exists in name only, and as long as it does what it is able to do it commits a mortal sin.

Once again the opening salvo is a categorical rejection of what the theologian of glory must maintain if there is to be room "to do our best." There must be some free will, no matter how minuscule. But the very claim is itself evidence of bondage over against the electing God. The fallen will cannot accept such a God. That is its bondage. The theologian of the cross, however, sees that that is exactly the problem, and therefore recognizes and confesses that, since the fall, free will does not exist in reality. It is an empty name. Perhaps it once existed, but no longer. Since this is the case, furthermore, when the fallen will sets out "to do its best," it commits deadly sin. This proposition is, of course, a mighty offense. We would normally admit that in doing our best we fall short of the goals we try to reach. But to say that even in trying we commit deadly or mortal sin seems outrageous. This thesis was perhaps the most offensive of all to the papal party in Luther's day. That is indicated by the fact that it was the only one from this Disputation actually attacked in the bull "Exsurge Domine" threatening Luther with excommunication. Luther's reply to the bull indicates how important he considered this thesis to be. He said it was "the highest and most important issue of our cause."[3]

After the fall, free will exists in name only and not in reality. How is this audacious claim to be understood? It is, of course, a very controversial and sensitive issue. We would think it to require a lengthy and involved discussion and demonstration. Luther's proof in the Disputation is very simple and brief, however. It is a direct conclusion from the fact, nature, and power of sin. The first part of the thesis, he insists, is evident because the fallen will is captive and subject to sin. "Not that it is nothing," he continues, "but that it is not free except to do evil." It is important to notice carefully what is being said here. There is indeed a will. We are willing beings. The will is not nothing. The problem is that it is not free but bound. We are not dealing here with determinism or fate. The will is not forced to do something "against its will." It is rather captive and

---

3. "Assertio omnium articulorum M. Lutheri per bullam Leonis X," WA 7.148.16.

thus bound to sin. The will does what it does because it wills to, and it will not do otherwise. The will is bound to will what it wills. After the fall, it is bound by sin, hence not free.

The scriptural authority Luther cites in this instance is John 8:34, 36, "Every one who commits sin is a slave to sin. . . . So if the Son makes you free, you will be free indeed." Further backup comes from St. Augustine, "Free will without grace has the power to do nothing but sin"[4] and "You call the will free, but in fact it is an enslaved will."[5] Sin makes it impossible for the will really to be called free because sin means an enslavement and bondage from which it is impossible for the will to escape. The self seeks its own self in all things, even in its piety. There is no way out. From this point of view the second part of the thesis is almost self-evident. It follows quite naturally that when the will, bound to its own self, tries to do its best, it only commits deadly sin. It commits deadly sin because it refuses to recognize the power of God to save and cuts off from grace. As we have pointed out in reference to the question of works, doing our best becomes a defense against the totality of grace. We refuse to live by the cross. Luther quotes Hosea 13:9, "Israel, you are bringing misfortune upon yourself, for your salvation is alone with me."

THESIS 14. Free will, after the fall, has power to do good only in a passive capacity, but it can always do evil in an active capacity.

Theses 14 and 15 are an attempt to define a little more closely what sort of ability may be ascribed to the will. If, as we have seen in

---

4. *The Spirit and the Letter* 3.5; *Patrologiae cursus completus*, ed. J. P. Migne (Paris, 1865), 44.203. (Hereafter cited as Migne.)
5. *Against Julian* 8.23; Migne 44.689.

thesis 13, the will is not nothing and is not forced or determined, and if, as we might say, we are not puppets, how then may the power of the will be described? If the claim is that we are to "do what is in us," then the question quite naturally follows: What then *is* in us? What sort of capacity do we have? To get at the question Luther here uses a distinction current in his day between what our translation has called a "passive capacity" and an "active capacity."[6] What does this mean? In its passive capacity the will can do good when *it is acted upon from without but not on its own, not in an active capacity.* A commonly used physical analogy is water. Water has a passive capacity to be heated, but it can't heat itself. It has no active capacity to do that.

The example Luther uses in his proof is even more to the point because it deals with death and life. On the one hand, corpses could be said to have a passive capacity for life because they can be raised from the dead. But not, of course, on their own power, not in an active capacity, not even in the slightest. Not even by doing their best! The capacity they have is strictly passive. They can be raised, but only by divine power. On the other hand, it is of course true that while a people live they have the active capacity to do something about life and death. They can take life, either their own or some other, but they can't create or give life. Yet that only demonstrates that, after the fall, will in its active capacity can only do evil. Since will after the fall is dead and bound to do deadly sin, it can be rescued only from without, as is indicated by the fact that it could not bring life out of death but could only be commanded from without by our Lord.

Thus, the fact that even after the fall the will is not nothing means that there is something there. What is it? It is a strictly passive capacity, not an active one. That means that *it can be*

---

6. In Latin, the distinction is between *potentia subjectiva* and *potentia activa.* WA 1.354.7-10.

changed but it will not change itself.[7] To be changed, it will have to be accessed "from without." But that will take radical action. It will take death and resurrection. So we are again pointed toward the cross.

> **THESIS 15.** Nor could free will remain in a state of innocence, much less do good, in an active capacity, but only in its passive capacity.

Scholastic teaching prior to the Reformation[8] tried to rescue some optimism in the understanding of human nature by claiming that at least before the fall there was some active capacity of free will to maintain the self in the state of innocence. This active capacity was apparently not considered potent enough to make progress toward the good, but it was at least strong enough to enable the creature to remain, to stand *(potuit stare),* in a state of innocence by virtue of the grace of creation. If there were not a "little bit" of such active capacity in the will, it was argued, how could Adam be held responsible for the fall? Thesis 15 rejects even this relatively mild attempt to establish some little toehold for free will and its works. Even *before the fall,* Luther insists, free will had no active capacity to remain in the state of innocence, but rather only a passive capacity.

7. The same position on the matter is reasserted in the debate with Erasmus in *The Bondage of the Will* (LW 33.67): "But if the power of free choice were said to mean that by which a man is capable of being taken hold of by the Spirit and imbued with the grace of God, as a being created for eternal life or death, no objection could be taken. For this power or aptitude, or as the Sophists say, this disposing quality or *passive aptitude,* we also admit; and who does not know that it is not found in trees or animals? For heaven, as the saying is, was not made for geese." Italics mine.

8. In this case, apparently, Luther has Peter Lombard in mind, as he points out in his proof.

That is to say, even before the fall Adam and Eve were upheld in the state of innocence not by their own power but from without. They remained strictly creatures who lived by faith and trusted in their creator and not their own power.

Although it may appear to be an obscure point, thesis 15 indicates clearly the kind of move a theologian of the cross will make when looking at the nature of our existence. The attempt to argue for at least a little bit of freedom in order to maintain human fault for the fall and sin is the telltale sign of the theologian of glory at work. Here that theology takes the form of claiming that at least before the fall Adam had the active capacity to persevere in the state of innocence. But is such a claim sufficient to maintain human responsibility and guilt? The questions tend eventually to rebound on God. Why could not God have given Adam the active capacity not only to stand in the state of innocence but also to progress toward the good? The problem, of course, is that if such an active capacity is ascribed to Adam before the fall, we run head-on into the claims that must also be made on behalf of grace. So the theologian of glory backs off and modestly claims just enough capacity in free will to make one guilty but not enough to do anything toward salvation. The assumption remains always the same. The way of works is the way of salvation. One needs help even before the fall, but more so afterward.

The theologian who "looks at all things through suffering and the cross" however, sees that this is just another instance of calling the bad good and the good bad. For what is the fall? It is precisely the attempt to claim something for the self and its works before God. To understand our relationship to God in terms of a scheme of law is exactly the mark of a fallen creation. To attempt to save even a little bit of such a scheme is simply to call the bad good.

Thus the theologian of the cross moves to close another door on the theology of glory. Even, or perhaps we should say *especially,* before the fall there is no active capacity either to stand or to progress in righteousness. Such an active capacity could only mean that the creature makes a move to be independent of the creator and sets out to create its own goodness. No good is done by the claim that without an active capacity of free will the creature cannot be held responsible because the problem is precisely that the fallen creature is blind to the true state of affairs. The fallen creature projects the scheme of works back before the fall and claims that responsibility can be accorded and measured only according to such a scheme. The theologian of glory then ends by equating what is really fallen existence with the state of innocence. The bad is called good and the good bad once again.

The cross spells the end of all such moves. Before the fall the creature lives by faith, trusting that creation is good and bending all effort toward taking care of it. The creature has only a passive capacity for the good, not an active one. That is, the creature is never meant to stand or operate alone but to be one through whom the creator works. The creature is turned about to take care of creation, to seek the good of the other, not of the self. To fall is precisely to be captivated, bound, seduced, and blinded by another vision, another hope, that of the active capacity of free will and its works. Responsibility for sin is never firmly established by such a scheme because we are blind to the original sin, the sin of independence from God, the sin of unfaithfulness parading as piety. True, we may confess to certain sins thereby but not to SIN. The sins we confess to in such cases are only peccadilloes, misdeeds, and failings according to the letter of the law — mostly the second table. They are, of course, serious enough, the source of guilt and anguish but more or less evident. When it comes to SIN, however, we have a deeper problem. As subsequent theses, particularly 19 and 20, will indicate, we are blind. It takes the cross to shock us, so to speak, into seeing. Only when that occurs will we begin to take responsibility for SIN.

THESIS 16. The person who believes that he can obtain grace by doing what is in him adds sin to sin so that he becomes doubly guilty.

Since we have now investigated the question of the potency of free will, the question of what actually is in us, thesis 16 returns to the attack on the idea that God will not fail to grant his grace to those who "do what is in them." Anyone who makes such a claim, Luther insists, adds sin to sin and becomes doubly guilty. All this follows quite naturally from what has already been said. The words of Luther's proof for this thesis are forthright and direct, a concise summary of the argument of the Disputation to this point:

> While a person is doing what is in him, he sins and seeks himself in everything. But if he should suppose that through sin he would become worthy of or prepared for grace, he would add haughty arrogance to his sin and not believe that sin is sin and evil is evil, which is an exceedingly great sin. As Jer. 2[:13] says, 'For my people have committed two evils: they have forsaken me, the fountain of living waters, and hewed out cisterns for themselves, broken cisterns, that can hold no water." That is, through sin they are far from God and yet they presume to do good by their own ability.[9]

But all of this is no doubt devastating to the theologian of glory. If we cannot be assured of grace by doing our best, and if our best only doubles sin, then what is the use? How shall we obtain grace at all? Luther's next paragraph in his proof indicates that he is well aware of the question. "Now you ask," he says, "What then shall we do? Shall we go our way with indifference because we can

9. LW 31.50.

do nothing but sin?" When such questions arise we have reached a critical point. The theologian of glory in us is beginning to cry out in frustration and despair! There is nothing to hold on to, no support left, nothing to do. Then the last-ditch defense is tried. "If all I do is sin, why not just quit? Why not just forget it all and sink into complete indifference?" At the last, the theologian of glory tries to force the hand of the theologian of the cross. The anticipated outcome is that the theologian of the cross should back off a bit and allow that little bit of operating room, the "comfort" of "doing what is in one."

Yet the theologian of the cross knows that there is nothing to do now but wait upon grace, to recognize that when all the supports have been cut away we can only throw ourselves on the mercy of God in Christ. So it is here in the second paragraph of the proof for thesis 16 and in the subsequent theses of the Disputation that the great turn to grace is finally made. For the first time (other than the incidental mention in thesis 9) Christ is spoken of in the Disputation. When the theologian of glory has finally bottomed out, Christ enters the scene as the bringer of salvation, hope, and resurrection. When the question, "Shall we go our way with indifference because we can do nothing but sin?" is finally raised, Luther replies,

> By no means. But having heard this, fall down and pray for grace and place your hope in Christ in whom is our salvation, life, and resurrection. For this reason we are so instructed — for this reason the law makes us aware of sin so that, having recognized our sin, we may seek and receive grace. Thus God "gives grace to the humble" [1 Pet. 5:5], and "whoever humbles himself will be exalted" [Matt. 23:12]. The law humbles, grace exalts. The law effects fear and wrath, grace effects hope and mercy. "Through the law comes knowledge of sin" [Rom. 3:20]; through knowledge of sin, however, comes humility; and through humility grace is acquired. Thus an action that is alien to God's nature results in

a deed belonging to his very nature: he makes a person a sinner so that he may make him righteous.[10]

This is Luther's answer to the incessant question in the Disputation about how one obtains grace: *by humility.* In other words, grace is acquired not by "doing what is in one." It is acquired when we are so completely humbled by God's alien work in law and wrath that we see how completely we are caught in the web of sin and turn to Christ as the only hope. "God gives grace to the humble" was a watchword of Augustinian — and Lutheran — theology.

Anyone who has some experience with these matters knows that the theologian of glory is not finished yet. For the question always comes back, "Isn't humbling oneself doing something?" Doesn't Luther's exhortation to "fall down and pray for grace and place your hope in Christ" mean we are "doing what it is in us"? There is always an attempt to keep a foot in the door! A more sophisticated complaint comes from historians and Luther scholars. They worry about whether Luther at this early stage in his thinking is not still caught in what is called Augustinian "humility piety," the idea that even if we cannot be saved by works, we can at least make it by humbling ourselves enough. In that case humility would tend to become a kind of work.

We cannot enter into all the ramifications of this complex debate here, but at least a couple of points ought to be stressed. First, it must be remembered that the mention of humility here comes at the end of the long debate in which Luther has systematically charged that every possible kind of work done by the self, whether pious or impious, is deadly sin. He could hardly be proposing now that there was some kind of work — even humility — that escaped this judgment. The humility Luther has in mind is in no way a human work. This is quite clear from the paragraph

10. LW 31.50-51.

quoted. In the terminology of the preceding debate we might say that humans have no active capacity to humble themselves but only a passive capacity. They can *be* humbled. Thus, in the proof quoted, humility is always something done to us. The instrument of this doing is the law and wrath, *God's* "alien work," not our pious posturing. Humility in this context means precisely to be reduced to the position where we claim *absolutely nothing.*[11]

One difficulty in this type of discussion, no doubt, is that precisely because the theology of glory reaches the end of the line, we too reach a limit in our use of language. Theology tries to describe accurately what the situation is, but in the fallen world descriptions always turn into prescriptions. Then they become deadly, especially when they turn up in sermons! So, talk of humility, or faith, or grace tends invariably to slip over into prescriptions for what we are to do to make ourselves as humble as possible, or to get some faith, or to decide for grace, and so on. In the theology of the cross, however, the point is that the language is to be used in such a way that every prescription is cut off. This is the significance of Luther's resort here to the way the language works. *The law humbles, grace exalts.* Something is done *to* us. There is probably no way to convince

11. There is an interesting marginal note on humility that unfortunately was not included in the American edition. It is appended however, in a footnote in the Library of Christian Classics edition. Scholars generally agree that it was added by Luther as late as 1545. It reads as follows: "This [i.e., the fact that the law makes sin known so that grace is sought] is indeed *the true humility* which is in utter despair of itself and hastens back to Christ in complete trust. This is the faith that saves. This embraces and precedes all merit. *This faith is the humility* which turns its back on its own reason and its own strength" (Martin Luther, *Early Theological Works*, edited and translated by James Atkinson, Library of Christian Classics, no. 16 [London: SCM Press; Philadelphia: Westminster, 1962], 289). Italics mine. The note is interesting in several respects. It seems to indicate that even at this very late date Luther still does not surrender the idea of humility. How could he, since it was a biblical teaching? However, the note may also indicate that he was concerned about clarifying, more than he had in 1518, the point that *faith* itself is the true humility, and thus removing the possibility of mistaking humility for a work.

theologians of glory that we are not doing something. Something must be done to them. We can only *be* humbled by the appropriate use of the language. The words must be law and gospel in such a way that there is no escape. Thus the impetuous question of whether or not humbling oneself or falling down and praying for grace is "doing something" can only be turned back on the questioner: "When you humble yourself and plead for grace, are you making the claim that you are doing something? If so, you are not pleading for grace, but only your own cause. And so you are still lost. Give up and believe the gospel!"

> **THESIS 17.** Nor does speaking in this man-
> ner give cause for despair, but for arousing
> the desire to humble oneself and seek the
> grace of Christ.

The natural protest of the theologian of glory against what has been said so far is that the theology of the cross is much too pessimistic, gloomy, and despairing. Must we not "accentuate the positive, eliminate the negative"? "Think positively?" Engage in "Possibility Thinking"? Is this not all too hard on our "self-esteem"? It is significant that in thesis 17 Luther has already anticipated that complaint. He insists that speaking as a theologian of the cross, telling it like it is, does not give cause for despair, but rather awakens the one thing that can help, the desire for the humility to seek the grace of Christ. It is important to see that the theologian of the cross moves to take up the question of despair only *after* hope in the grace of Christ has been announced.

Theologians of glory can never quite understand this. Bound to the accomplishments and works of the self, theologians of glory can only look on the idea that "doing one's best" is mortal sin or that one who puts trust in such doing only adds sin on sin as hopelessly negative and pessimistic. Theologians of glory are trapped in the "merit machine," and thus can fight despair only by falling back on their accomplishments. That can only mean that they are doomed to ultimate despair because sin never stops and no amount of works can counterbalance it. To use again the analogy of addiction, when the optimistic encouragement to quit fails, it only increases despair and fosters hypocrisy. For the alcoholic the humility to confess, "I am an alcoholic," is not a mark of despair but of hope. It is false optimism that brings ultimate despair. There is an interesting passage in Luther's early treatise on Psalms (*The Operationes in Psalmos,* 1519-1521) that ferrets out the real cause of ultimate despair:

> The cause of despair is not the multitude or magnitude of the sins, but the wrong affection in those who seek after good works in the time of their trouble of conscience, in order to set them against their sins as a counterbalance and satisfaction. For such imagine . . . that their sins have been and can be overcome by such works: and therefore, not being able to find the victory after which they labor, and not knowing that they ought to turn to the mercy of God, desperation of necessity follows.[12]

In the proof for this thesis Luther uses the analogy of speaking to the sick. One does not give cause for despair if one warns sick people of the seriousness of their illness and urges them to see a doctor for a cure. Despair would rather come if one is falsely optimistic and tells them that they don't need a physician while they steadily decline toward death. We see here again how remarkably realistic and unsentimental the theologian of the cross is. The theologian of the cross knows that we do the world no good by playing the role of pious or sentimental optimists. One must "say what a thing is." One is given the courage to be honest.

12. WA 5.159.16-21. Lenker, 258.

THESIS 18. It is certain that man must utterly despair of his own ability before he is
prepared to receive the grace of Christ.

This thesis completes the section (13-18) on the question of whether
the will has any real desire or capacity to prepare itself to receive
the grace of Christ. Consequently, it is the final conclusion and the
straight answer to the question with which the section has been
dealing: How then are we prepared to receive the grace of Christ?
We must utterly despair of our own ability. The thesis states the
matter categorically. "It is certain." It is not a matter for conjecture.
As the foregoing discussion has insisted again and again, we must
not to any degree whatsoever place our trust in "doing our best,"
or "doing what is in us," or doing just that "little bit," and so forth.
The proof for the thesis reiterates the rationale:

> He who acts simply in accordance with his ability and believes
> that he is thereby doing something good does not seem worthless
> to himself, nor does he despair of his own strength. Indeed, he is
> so presumptuous that he strives for grace in reliance on his own
> strength.[13]

The law, on the other hand, won't allow such presumption:

> The law wills that man despair of his own ability, for it leads him
> into hell and makes him a poor man and shows him that he is a
> sinner in all his works, as the Apostle does in Rom. 2 and 3[:9],
> where he says, "I have already charged that all men are under the
> power of sin."[14]

13. LW 31.52.
14. LW 31.51-52.

Now one cannot help but notice that there is something of a problem in the relation between thesis 17 and 18. Thesis 17 states that the honest speaking of the previous thesis, which rejects "doing what is in one" does not give cause for despair. Thesis 18, on the other hand, announces that "man must utterly despair of his own ability" to be properly prepared. Quite obviously there are different nuances at work here in the use of "despair." It is important to sort them out to understand what Luther means when he speaks about the matter. I have tried to anticipate this in speaking of "ultimate despair" in some of the comments on thesis 17. When, as theologians of glory, we think our own works are the only way out, we get trapped by our own sins. Then we are without hope and on the way to ultimate despair, the despair, say, of a Judas. "If only I had not done it!" "There is no hope for me." Despair becomes ultimate. The cause of such ultimate despair is that we are still trapped in a false regard for our works — so much so, perhaps, that in a kind of perverse pride we think that not even the grace of God can blot out our failures! The implication is that by avoiding sin we could better our status in God's sight. Regard for our own ability is still the presumption by which we operate. But then we have not *utterly despaired* of our own ability. We have not surrendered the belief that we manufacture our own destiny by "doing what is in us."

The "utter despair of one's own ability" of thesis 18 is not the "ultimate despair" of one still caught in the trap of presumption, but rather a despair that is "preparation to receive the grace of Christ." Indeed, we can say, utter despair of our own ability is not something we achieve on our own. It is not a new "doing what is in one." It is itself possible only because the grace of Christ has brought new hope. So it is that preaching against our own ability in these matters does not give cause for despair because it seeks to prevent the ultimate despair that will inevitably result if we rely on those abilities. At the same time it is true that such preaching brings about the final surrender of faith in self, the "utter despair of our own ability" that is inspired by and prepares to receive the grace of Christ. Ultimate despair is due to the temptation to believe that there is no hope beyond our own abilities. Despair itself then becomes ultimate and so leads to death. Utter despair of our own ability, however, looks to the grace of Christ and so leads to life. This subtle nuance points to a fundamental theological divide.

III

The Great Divide: The Way of Glory versus the Way of the Cross

THESES 19-24

In theses 19 to 24 we come to the keystone of the great arch spanning the cleft between the law of God (thesis 1) and the love of God (thesis 28). Theses 19-24 are the most commented on of all the theses of the Heidelberg Disputation and are usually the centerpiece of any discussion on the theology of the cross. This is one of the few times Luther explicitly uses the actual words designating the theology of the cross as a particular way of doing theology in contrast to the theology of glory. So theses 19-24 get a lot of attention in treatises on the theology of the cross. Unfortunately what usually happens then is that these theses are taken out of their context in the Disputation and treated as though they were to stand by themselves as a more or less discrete theological program or treatise on the knowledge of God according to the theology of the cross and such matters.[1]

Such procedure runs the risk of missing important connections. In the first place, the great divide between the theologian of

1. See Vercruysse, "Gesetz und Liebe," 29.

69

glory and the theologian of the cross is a direct consequence of the argument to this point. The question of the knowledge of God is directly related to the claim that we can, by our natural powers, prepare for grace by "doing what is in us." "Doing what is in ourselves" by natural ability or trying to hold to the efficacy of such doing before God *presumes* a natural knowledge of God's justifying action. It presupposes a certain way of knowing and seeing God. A fault in the estimation of works (part 1) is based on a false estimate of the power of will (part 2), which in turn presumes a knowledge of God's judgment on such works (part 3). They are just links in the same chain. Thus the entire discussion to this point leads to an unavoidable theological divide. Theses 19-24 set forth this divide, which is usually missed when we take the theses out of context.

Second, treating theses 19-24 by themselves tends also to miss the fact that when we arrive at this point in the Disputation, the theologian has come to a real existential crisis. At stake is not merely a theology, whether it be of the cross or something else. At stake is the very survival and viability of the *theologian*. Thesis 17 and 18 concluded the discussion to this point by raising the issue of despair. Thesis 18 insisted that "it is certain" we must "utterly despair of our own ability" if we are to be properly prepared for grace. The question now is how we as *theologians* are going to move. If "doing what is in us" presupposes a certain natural knowledge of God, where does "utterly despairing of our own ability" lead? What moves will we who so despair make? Will we as theologians betray what has been said so far? Will we even be worthy of the name? That is the question now. So it is vital to note that in these theses Luther does not talk much about *theology*. Rather, he talks about *theologians and how they respond to the crisis*. He points out how they operate, how what they hold about works and willing determines how and where they expect to find and know God.

When we move to look at theses 19-24, a certain structure of comparison and contrast is again obvious.[2] The great divide is marked out clearly. There are two kinds of theologians, theologians of glory and theologians of the cross. The theses basically set forth the contrast in the way the two operate. The theses can thus be divided into two groups of three: theses 19-21 deal with the way the theologian operates, while theses 22-24 deal with the improper and proper use of wisdom and law.

In 19-20, once again, an exact parallel of opposites is obvious. In thesis 21 the outcome of the opposition is stated within the thesis. This yields a structure as follows (translating somewhat freely):

The Theologian of Glory	The Theologian of the Cross
Thesis 19	*Thesis 20*
1. That person does not deserve to be called a theologian	1. But [that person deserves to be called a theologian]
2. Who claims to see into the invisible things of God	2. Who comprehends what is visible of God *(visibilia et posteriora Dei)*
3. By seeing through earthly things (events, works).	3. Through suffering and the cross.
Thesis 21	
4. The theologian of glory calls evil good and good evil.	4. The theologian of the cross says what a thing is.

Once again note carefully that the immediate focus is on theologians and their mode of operating, not on theology as such. The great divide is first of all in the way they look for God in the world, in their "seeing" (19, 20), then secondly and consequently in their speaking (21). Faulty or misdirected sight results in false speaking.

2. Again I follow the analysis of Vercruysse, "Gesetz und Liebe," 29-30.

THESIS 19. That person does not deserve to be called a theologian who looks upon the invisible things of God as though they were clearly perceptible in those things that have actually happened (or have been made, created).[3]

How is the great divide to be described? Luther begins by asserting that there is a fundamental presumption about "sight" involved — so fundamental indeed that those who so presume do not really deserve to be called theologians. We might call them philosophers or moralists or metaphysicians or even ethicists, perhaps, but hardly theologians. Actually, of course, Luther does concede the title (thesis 21) but qualifies it by calling them "theologians of glory" in contrast to "theologians of the cross." This is the shorthand way of designating the great divide.

How do theologians of glory operate differently from theologians of the cross? That is the issue for this section of the Disputation. Theologians of glory operate on the assumption that creation and history are transparent to the human intellect, that one can *see through* what is made and what happens so as to peer into the "invisible things of God." There is a kind of oxymoron in the thesis in speaking of "seeing the invisible," but it is intended, no doubt, to indicate the presumption involved. How do we see the invisible?

---

3. There is an ongoing debate about the translation of the final clause of this thesis, *ea, quae facta sunt,* literally, "those things that have been made." Does "have been made" here refer to creation? If so, then the knowledge of God that Luther intended would be that gained by analogy from creation. But elsewhere in the Disputation the argument centers more on the attempt to mount up to God via human works, as in thesis 22. The translation of LW is ambiguous, no doubt intentionally, so I have added a parenthetical clause. I have tried in my comments to encompass both possibilities by suggesting that the "knowledge" the theologian of glory arrives at can be understood as both divine perfections and therefore also goals for human "works."

Obviously we can't, directly. However, theologians of glory work, as one would say today, by analogy. The assumption is that the visible creation yields clues, if not directly at least by analogy, to what is invisible in God, to the nature and logic of God. We can, that is, figure out something of what God is like by looking at the world he has made and how it works. The "invisible things of God" we can supposedly "see" by this mode of operation are, in Luther's mind, such things as "virtue, godliness, wisdom, justice, goodness, and so forth."[4] They seem to be a collection of those things humans are to strive for and that find their perfection in God, essences and qualities, both divine perfections and therefore also human goals. The claim to be able to "see" in that sense would lead to the assumption that we could set up a way to God. There would be, so to speak, a glory road, which should eventually lead to God.

But why should one who operates in that fashion not deserve to be called a theologian? Is this not the business of theology, to figure out the logic of God and his action in the world? This is precisely where the great divide becomes apparent. One who proposes to "see through" creation and divine action actually ends by dissolving the power of the cross in a sea of abstract universals and consequently undercutting the present actuality of the word of the cross. Our "theologians," that is, undermine the very proclamation they are supposed to foster and so forfeit their right to the title. Perhaps an example will help to make this audacious claim more clear. Theologians from time immemorial down to the present have worried about divine attributes like timelessness and immutability, attributes of divine majesty. They seem to cancel out the freedom and responsibility of the creature, especially when questions about election and predestination are raised. If God immutably elects "before all time," how can there be freedom? So what do theologians do? They go to work with philosophical presuppositions to solve,

4. LW 31.52.

remove, or in some way explain away the problem of objectionable attributes.[5] They think, that is, that they are able to see into the invisible things of God through the things that are made.

But what is accomplished thereby? First, it can be observed that it never seems to work. The attributes of divine majesty keep coming back like a song. The attempt to do something about them has to be redone, it seems, by every new generation. We never seem quite convinced by the theology. Theologians, you might say, are like Sisyphus, condemned in Hades to rolling a huge stone up the hill, only to have it constantly roll back down. Incidentally, it is interesting to note that Sisyphus was condemned in that manner because he had discovered some of the secrets of Zeus! Second, even if such attempts were to succeed, theology would only make God ludicrous. For what is God without the attributes of divine majesty? No doubt that is why we sense something is amiss, and the stone keeps rolling back down to crush us.

Third, and most importantly, all that such theology accomplishes in the end is to pull the rug out from under the proclamation. This is the ultimate reason why those who operate in this manner do not deserve the title "theologian." What they do is, of course, easily enough done. But the radical nature of works like the Heidelberg Disputation is to expose the fact that it is not a neutral or harmless enterprise. Those who indulge in it never seem to understand that there is no abstract theological solution to the problem

---

5. This has been attempted in ways too numerous to mention here. It has long been the favorite parlor game of philosophers and theologians. Generally speaking, among theologians who wish to preserve at least the facade of Christianity, it appears to happen in one of two ways: either Jesus and his cross are taken into the divine, that is, they assume the character of "timeless truth" of a philosophical sort available to our choices; or, more recently, the divine is collapsed into time in the event of Jesus and the cross. "Timelessness" and "immutability" and such "masks" of God (as Luther would have called them) are supposedly removed. Of course, the question remains to haunt us: Do they really go away at the fancy of the philosopher/theologian? Can theology actually pull the mask from the face of the hidden God?

of the divine majesty. The only solution is the cross itself and the subsequent proclamation of the word of the cross as a divine deed, the work of the Spirit, in the living present. That is to say, as fallen creatures and not creators we will *always* be threatened by God, who is hidden by the masks of divine majesty. Like conscience they will never go away and stay away. They are always there, always ready to attack. They don't submit to manipulation. The only refuge is the word of the cross in the here and now. Through the *preaching* of the cross in the living present, not through theological explanations, we are defended from the terror of the divine majesty. Precisely against the threat of supposed divine timelessness and immutability we are claimed in the concrete word of the cross in the living present; through baptism and Supper we are washed and fed. We feel and taste the truth in the here and now. To believe means precisely to be claimed by the cross and its word, to cling to that and find one's assurance there. The "solution" to the problem of God, that is, is not in the classroom but in church. When theologians do not grasp that, or when they forget it, they no longer deserve the title. In spite of grand and high-sounding theologies, they will likely just undercut the church's task. There is a great divide here. To be grasped by that fact is to be on the way to becoming a theologian of the cross.

On the other side of the divide, however, is the temptation always to operate on the assumption that we can see through the divine masks to the divine majesty. That is, of course, the presupposition necessary to the claim that we can prepare for grace by doing our best with our natural powers. For the most part we will, no doubt, be modest enough to admit that we cannot go the whole way on the glory road without the help of grace. But then Christ gets called into the scheme to make it work. Christ and the cross are taken up into abstract doctrines. The result is that the cross too is looked upon as though it were transparent. Theologians of glory will claim not only to be able to see through creation but also to *see through* the cross to figure out the final "Why." Why did Jesus have to die? Apparently to pay for our failures and mistakes in the pursuit of "virtue, godliness, wisdom, justice, goodness, and so forth." Thus, the cross is not really just what is visible. It becomes a launching pad for speculative flights into intellectual space, into the invisible things of God. It is not simply that a man sent from God is suffering, forsaken, and dying at our hands — as if that were not enough! — but he is a payment to God (whose justice one has supposedly peered into and figured out) in some celestial court transaction.

Theologians of glory are thus always driven to seek transcendent meaning, to try to see into the invisible things of God, to get a line on the logic of God. They look at the cross and ask, "What is it all about?" They wonder what is "behind" it all. There is a reason for this, of course. If we can *see through* the cross to what is supposed to be behind it, we don't have to *look at* it! It is, finally, a matter of self-defense. He was "as one from whom men hide their faces" (Isa. 53:3). If the cross can be neatly folded into the scheme of the self's glory road, it will do no harm.

Luther apparently does not think it necessary at this point to spend much time refuting this position. The proof he offers for this thesis is among the shortest of the Disputation. Perhaps he assumes that by now the presumption inherent in the position ought to be obvious. At any rate, he contents himself simply with pointing to Romans 1:22, where St. Paul speaks of those who claim to be wise but are nevertheless fools. The context of the Romans passage should perhaps be filled out a bit. The fools are they who knew God but "did not honor him *as God* or give thanks to him but became futile *in their thinking* and their senseless minds were darkened. Claiming to be wise they became fools" (Rom. 1:21-22).

How shall fools be made wise? The problem is that at the deepest level we have here not just a set of teachings, theological opinion, or that which we might take or leave at will and which might be corrected by better information, but *temptation*. As we have already indicated, it is a matter finally of self-defense. Thus the proof concludes with just a brief parting shot about the uselessness of this method of operation in making one either worthy or wise. Peering into the "invisible things of God" only "puffs up, blinds, and hardens" (cf. thesis 22). Luther's indication of what such invisible things might be has already been given: virtue, godliness, wisdom, justice, goodness, and so forth. Knowledge of divine essences and qualities, Luther asserts, does not make wise men out of fools. Indeed, it is more likely to make fools out of the wise! Essences and qualities are abstractions; they are what is left when all the action, particularly the suffering and the dying, has been stripped away. There is a fundamental misdirection in seeing. Our theologians must be taught where to look and what to see. That leads to thesis 20.

> **THESIS 20.** That person deserves to be called a theologian, however, who comprehends the visible and manifest things of God through suffering and the cross.

Theologians of the cross see things differently. They can't get around the cross. They can't see through the cross to what is "behind" it. They can't escape the realization that virtue, godliness, wisdom, justice, goodness, and so forth are exactly what put Jesus on the cross. The cross is not transparent but more like a mirror. Our line of sight is bent back upon itself, upon ourselves and our world. We "see," so to speak, in the reflected light of the cross. Instead of trying to see through the world and the cross to the invisible things of God, we are turned back to what is "visible and manifest" of God here among us, and we "comprehend" it through suffering and the cross.[6] Suffering and the

---

6. The Latin original of theses 19 and 20 has a chiasm that neatly expresses the difference in what our theologians look at and what they see. The chiasm is difficult

cross become the key to the comprehension of one who deserves the title of theologian.

What is meant here by the "visible and manifest things of God"? The Latin original furnishes a hint as to what Luther had in mind. The word here translated as "manifest" is *posteriora*. It means "back" or "hinder parts." This indicates that the discussion is intended to call to mind the event in Exodus 33:18-23 in which Moses asks to see God's glory — even Moses has the aspirations of a theologian of glory! God tells Moses that no one can see God's face and live. Consequently Moses is to hide in a cleft in the rock when God approaches. God covers Moses' eyes and allows him to see only his back, the *posteriora*, as he passes by. God, that is, actually prevents Moses from seeing his glory. To be sure, that is on the one hand a gracious act since no one can look on God's face and live. But for a theologian of glory it is on the other hand a supreme put-down. God won't let even Moses see what every theologian of glory so desperately wants to see. God allows Moses to see only his back when he has passed by. In Luther's mind here it is the suffering, despised, and crucified Jesus that takes the place of God's backside. No doubt Luther uses this somewhat offensive image precisely to shock the theologian of glory in us. This comes out in his proof for this thesis:

> The manifest and visible things of God are placed in opposition to the invisible, namely, his human nature, weakness, foolishness. The Apostle in 1 Cor. 1[:25] calls them the weakness and folly of God. Because men misused the knowledge of God through works, God wished again to be recognized in suffering, and to

---

to translate into English. The "seeing" of thesis 19 is *intellecta conspicit*, whereas that of thesis 20 is *conspecta intelligit*. Perhaps one could say that the theologian of glory of thesis 19 contemplates the invisible intellectually, whereas the theologian of the cross of thesis 20 comprehends the visible contemplatively (through suffering and the cross).

condemn wisdom concerning invisible things by means of the wisdom concerning visible things, so that those who did not honor God as manifested in his works should honor him as he is hidden in his suffering.[7]

God refuses to be seen in any other way, both for our protection and to put down the theologian of glory in us. Theologians of the cross are therefore those whose eyes have been turned away from the quest for glory by the cross, who have eyes only for what is visible, what is actually there to be seen of God, the suffering and despised crucified Jesus. It was the pagan Pilate who said it: *Ecce Homo!* Behold the man! Faulty eyesight is to be corrected by the cross.

Correcting the sight of the theologian of glory is a drastic business. In his proof Luther uses language taken from St. Paul (quoting Isaiah) in 1 Corinthians 1:19, "I will destroy the wisdom of the wise. . . ." The cross therefore is actually intended to destroy the sight of the theologian of glory. In the cross God actively hides himself. God simply refuses to be known in any other way.

> As the Apostle says in 1 Cor. 1[:21], "For since, in the wisdom of God, the world did not know God through wisdom, it pleased God through the folly of what we preach to save those who believe." Now it is not sufficient for anyone, and it does him no good to recognize God in his glory and majesty, unless he recognizes him in the humility and shame of the cross. Thus God destroys the wisdom of the wise, as Isa. [45:15] says, "Truly thou are a God who hidest thyself."[8]

The cross cannot be considered therefore as one option among several in our attempts to see God. The cross shuts down alternatives.

7. LW 31.52.
8. LW 31.52-53.

It destroys the wisdom of the wise. It blinds the sight of the theologian of glory. What is revealed is precisely that we don't know God. Our problem is not that we lay claim to such little knowledge of God but that we think we know so much. So God hides from us. As with Moses, he puts his hand over our eyes. God refuses to be known according to the schemes of a theology of glory. What is vital here is absolute concentration on the rejected, crucified Jesus.

> So also in John 14[:8], where Philip spoke according to the theology of glory: "Show us the Father." Christ forthwith set aside his flighty thought about seeing God elsewhere and let to himself, saying, "Philip, he who has seen me has seen the Father" [John 14:9]. *For this reason true theology and recognition of God are in the crucified Christ, as it is also stated in John 10 [John 14:6]: "No one comes to the Father, but by me." "I am the door" [John 10:9], and so forth.*[9]

Theologians of the cross are those from whom all support other than the cross has simply been torn away. The situation is not that we might sit back and upon reflection calmly choose to be this or that sort of theologian. If we look *at* it instead of *through* it or *behind* it, the cross tears away all other possibilities. So as theologians of the cross we operate on the premise that faith in the crucified and risen one is all we have going for us. All the supports of the theology of glory are destroyed by the cross. The cross is the end result of the theology of glory. So it is finished. There are no escape hatches. By faith we become a human being, a person of this world, a truly historical being, because there is nothing to do now but wait, hope, pray, and trust in the promise of him who nevertheless conquers, the crucified and risen Jesus. By faith we are simply *in Christ,* waiting to see what will happen to and in us. As Luther could put it in his

9. LW 31.53.

most famous saying in the commentary on the first twenty-two Psalms from about this time, "The cross alone is our theology" *(CRUX sola est nostra Theologia)*.[10] More must be said about this, but for now we turn to our next thesis.

THESIS 21. A theology of glory calls evil good and good evil. A theology of the cross calls the thing what it actually is.

This is the way the thesis reads in the earlier printings of the American edition of *Luther's Works*. I use the translation purposely here as a kind of object lesson. The Latin original speaks not of a *theology* of glory or of the cross, but, as we have been insisting all along, of a *theologian*. Later printings have, fortunately, made this correction. But the mistake illustrates a persistent tendency. Our temptation is always to change the subject. In this case the blame is switched from us to theology. The assumption is that we can more or less easily escape the error described by just disavowing the theology. "Call evil good and good evil? Who? Me? No way! I don't hold with the theology of glory!" So the matter is settled — supposedly. Yet we have seen all along in the preceding theses and their proofs how we actually do get drawn into calling evil good and good evil. The theologian is the culprit here, not the theology as such. The theologian is always the acting subject, indeed, the ultimate reason why the theology comes out as it does. The point here is that the theologian of glory is *impelled* to act in a certain way. We can even say that over against the cross all theologize as they *must*. This is the outcome of the great divide. Faulty seeing leads inexorably to false speaking. The cross, as Luther could put it, finds us out *(Crux probat omnia)*.[11]

10. WA 5.176.32.
11. WA 5.179.31. Lenker, 294-95.

The theologian of glory calls evil good and good evil. A theologian of the cross calls a thing what it is. The great divide in seeing leads to a completely different way of speaking. It leads to plain and honest talk about what we do and what happens to us. The theologian of glory has all the value signs exactly reversed. How can we grasp this? Previously we have seen how the value signs are reversed with reference to works that we do. Here, however, a deeper dimension opens before us, one of the most profound and difficult dimensions of what being a theologian of the cross involves: how we speak of and cope with suffering. Before we hurry to comment, we must listen to Luther's words in his proof for this thesis:

> This is clear: He who does not know Christ does not know God hidden in suffering. Therefore he prefers works to suffering, glory to the cross, strength to weakness, wisdom to folly, and, in general, good to evil. These are the people whom the Apostle calls "enemies of the cross of Christ" [Phil. 3:18], for they hate the cross and suffering and love works and the glory of works. Thus they call the good of the cross evil and the evil of a deed good. God can be found only in suffering and the cross, as has already been said. Therefore the friends of the cross say that the cross is good and works are evil, for through the cross works are dethroned and the Old Adam, who is especially edified by works, is crucified. It is impossible for a person not to be puffed by his good works unless he has first been deflated and destroyed by suffering and evil until he knows that he is worthless and that his works are not his but God's.[12]

Direct, plain, clear, entirely unsentimental, but for that reason difficult and offensive words. What we have to say about suffering is usually a prime example of the faulty speech of the theologian of

12. LW 31.53.

glory. Suffering is called evil and works good. The word of the cross, however, *inflicts* the very suffering they talked about. The words are difficult just for the reason Luther says they are. We are inveterate theologians of glory. We are tempted and bound to be so. We invest all our capital in works. There is then a necessary relation between works and the way we regard suffering. We work to *avoid* suffering — mostly for here but sometimes also for the hereafter. Or, if we don't work to avoid suffering, we run from it. We might even work to stave off the fear of death, not to say the suffering of hell. We depend upon and glory in our works, and we call these self-serving deeds good. Suffering, we insist, is bad. If it comes upon us we immediately begin to wonder if we have failed somehow in our works. Since theologians of glory shy away from the depths of the cross and its forgiveness, there can be no honesty about reality and the way things are. The self that invests in its own works has no recourse but to defend itself to the end.

As a result we look on suffering from the outside. It is painful and generally to be avoided. From this position of Olympian transcendence we may on occasion feel guilty enough to descend into the world of suffering to express our solidarity with the oppressed, the poor, and the afflicted. We will call it "Incarnational Theology" or something of the sort. (Notice how easily one can slip over into calling it a theology! Then one can espouse it without doing much. One can take occasional trips to impoverished or ravaged areas and come home to talk about it.) Jesus is set up as our model. "Misery loves company" is the prime Christological motif. Christ humbled himself and descended into the world of suffering so we ought to too. If, on occasion, this causes a bit of pain or discomfort, we can tally it up on our ledger of good works.

Thus theologians of glory are not above turning even "The Theology of the Cross" to their own advantage. So it can even happen as we see today that "The Theology of the Cross" comes into a certain vogue. It provides additional levers for therapists and ethicists.[13] As a "theology," the theology of the cross turns very easily into a negative theology of glory. Our occasional pain becomes our good work. If we can't make it by escaping suffering, perhaps we can by entering into it. So we hear a good bit of sentimental talk these days about entering into solidarity with those who suffer, as though it were something we might do on weekends.

Contemporary theologians talk much about the problem of evil. Some think it is the most difficult problem for theology today and one of the most persistent causes of unbelief. One wonders, however, just how much this is itself the result of the faulty speech of the theology of glory. Since suffering is itself classified as evil, it is of course simply lumped together with disaster, crime, misfortune of every sort, abuse, holocaust, and all manner of notorious wrong as one and the same problem. So it is almost universally the case that theologians and philosophers *include* suffering without further qualification among those things they call evil. Of course there are different sides to the question. Evil does cause suffering — but not always. Indeed, the usual complaint is that the evil don't seem to suffer. However, the causes of suffering may not always be evil — perhaps not even most of the time. Love can cause suffering. Beauty can be the occasion for suffering. Children with their demands and impetuous cries can cause suffering. Just the toil and trouble of daily life can cause suffering, and so on. Yet these are surely not to be termed evil. The problem of suffering should not just be rolled up with the problem of evil. Only false speaking lures us into doing that.

Identification of suffering with evil has the further result that God must be absolved from all blame.[14] Thus, the theologian of

13. See, for instance, the article by Larry Rasmussen, "Returning to Our Senses: The Theology of the Cross as a Theology for Eco-justice," in *After Nature's Revolt: Eco-Justice and Theology*, edited by Dieter T. Hessel (Minneapolis: Fortress, 1992).

14. It is remarkable that there were so few attempts to construct theodicies prior to the 18th century. Certainly there was no shortage of suffering and disaster. Life was

glory adds to the perfidy of false speech by trying to assure us that God, of course, has nothing to do with suffering and evil. God is "good," the rewarder of all our "good" works, the pot of gold at the end of the rainbow of merit. But is this prettified God the God of the Bible? Is it not quite probable that just these attempts to whitewash God are the cause of unbelief?[15] Meanwhile, suffering goes on unabated. If God has nothing to do with suffering, what is he involved with? Whoever does not know God hidden in suffering, Luther asserts in his proof, does not know God at all.

The result of false speech is that attitudes toward suffering today are fraught with ambiguity. On the one hand, suffering is virtually identified with the problem of evil. Some, perhaps mainly feminist theologians today, launch a polemic against the cross claiming that in it Christianity glorifies suffering. A Father-God who demands the suffering of his Son is guilty of "divine child abuse"! Suffering, it is claimed, is never redemptive.[16] On the other hand,

------

"nasty, brutish, and short." In Luther's own day the black death had decimated the population of Europe and still threatened. Villages and towns lived in constant dread of fire and natural disasters, and so forth. Yet attempts to absolve God were deemed foolish. Is it not curious that only when life seems to be easier do thinkers set out to "justify" God. Is it perhaps that when we think ourselves to have done so well we question God for being so inept? Perhaps it is as Hannah Arendt remarks, "When men could no longer *praise,* they turned their greatest conceptual efforts to *justifying* God and His Creation in theodicies" (Hannah Arendt, *The Life of the Mind,* vol. 2, *Willing* [New York: Harcourt Brace Jovanovich, 1977], 97).

15. James Turner believes that to be the case. See his penetrating work, *Without God, Without Creed: The Origins of Unbelief in America* (Baltimore: Johns Hopkins University Press, 1985). Turner indicates that it was precisely the attempt on the part of theologians and preachers to accommodate God to current modes of thought that led to unbelief, not the fear that God was truly God in majestic awesomeness. God was turned into a patsy not worthy of commanding belief.

16. See Joanne Carlson Brown and Rebecca Parker, "For God so Loved the World?" in *Christianity, Patriarchy and Abuse, A Feminist Critique,* edited by Joanne Carlson Brown and Carole R. Bohn (New York: The Pilgrim Press, 1989), 1-29. The claim that suffering is *never* redemptive is surely somewhat shortsighted. To live, to love, to care, to be concerned about others will mean, certainly, to suffer in one way

from much the same point of view, a negative theology of glory decrees that we ought to enter into solidarity with suffering. If we can't escape it, we can still use it to our advantage. There is even much talk about the suffering of God in this vein. God makes himself "vulnerable" in Jesus, so we ought to too. Misery loves company.

In the face of all this, the claim here is that it is only *through suffering and the cross* that sinners can see and come to know God. So theologians of the cross must be able to speak honestly and forthrightly, to "say what a thing is." This suffering is from God and it is good. That is the deepest reason why we call the Friday of the crucifixion *good.* But now we must be careful. What is meant by suffering here? It seems obvious that Luther does not mean just physical pain. He himself experienced much excruciating pain during his life, but never to my knowledge does he identify that pain with the suffering worked by the cross or use it to make claims for himself as a sufferer. For Luther the sufferings of the spirit, the pangs of conscience, the terrors of temptation *(Anfechtungen),* were always more agonizing and serious than the physical pain he also knew well. Even physical death, though heartrending enough for loved ones, was a far lesser matter than the kind of death experienced when the wrath of God assaults the sinner.

So the suffering Luther has in mind first and foremost is the result of God's operation on the sinner. One can find reference to that throughout his writings.[17] The suffering Luther has in mind

---

or another. Even to write controversial articles and have to bear the criticism and even scorn that follow will mean, no doubt, to suffer! And one hopes, I expect, that it will be in some small measure redemptive.

17. The exposition of the Psalms 1–22 from roughly this same time (*Operationes in Psalmos, 1519-1521,* WA 5) contains countless instances in which suffering is the result of the divine action in reducing works and merits to naught. The following are some good examples: "Other virtues may be perfected by doing; *but faith, hope, and love, only by suffering,* by suffering I say, that is, *by being passive under the divine operation*" (WA 5.176.1); "The soul is taken hold of [by the pure Word of God] and

is something God inflicts on us just by virtue of the fact that he moves against the presumption of our works. He is out to do it all. We *suffer* this unilateral action of God. We suffer because we don't like it. We don't like to be put out of control. It means that we are rendered totally *passive* by the divine operation through the cross and resurrection of Jesus. "Passive" has, of course, become something of a bad word in contemporary speech. It is taken to mean lack of assertiveness, lack of motivation, lack of care, extreme lassitude. But we should recall that it comes from the same root as "passion" and means literally the same thing as suffering — as in "the passion of our Lord." Luther used it constantly to describe the proper disposition of the sinner to the grace of God. Precisely because the sinner has taken up an active position (the "active potency" of thesis 14!) in relation to God's activity on the basis of works, God's action over against the sinner can only result in suffering. The sinner is therefore rendered absolutely passive, put totally out of commission, we might say today. The sinner can only *suffer* the divine action. The comment on Psalm 2:9, "Thou shalt break them with a rod of iron," gives a good picture of the kind of suffering Luther has in mind:

---

does not take hold of anything itself; that is, it is stripped of its own garments, of its shoes, of all its possessions, and of all its imaginations, and is taken away by the Word . . . into the wilderness . . . to invisible things, into the vineyard, and into the marriage chamber. But this leading, this taking away, and this stripping, miserably tortures [the soul]. For it is a hard path to walk in, and a straight and narrow way, to leave all visible things, to be stripped of all natural senses and ideas, and to be led out of all those things to which we have been accustomed; this, indeed, is to die, and to descend into hell" (WA 5.176.16-24). Luther knows of course, that such passages have the ring of mysticism about them. So he goes on a bit later to criticize mysticism for understanding the matter as "elicited acts," that is, as something we do: "They do not believe them to be the sufferings and feeling sensations of the cross, death, and hell. The CROSS alone is our theology" (WA 5.176.32). It is significant that the last sentence so often quoted is directed precisely against a theology tempted to turn the suffering involved into something to do rather than something done to us.

For since the Word of Christ is the Word not in the flesh but in the spirit, it must suppress and cast out the salvation, peace, life, and grace of the flesh. When it does this, it appears to the flesh harder and more cruel than iron itself. For whenever a carnal man is touched in a wholesome way by the Word of God, one thing is felt, but another actually happens. Thus it is written [1 Sam. 2:6-7]: "The Lord kills and brings to life; He brings down to hell and raises up; He brings low, He also exalts." Isaiah also beautifully portrays this allegorical working of God when he says [28:21], "He does His work — strange is His deed; and He works His work — alien is His work!" It is as if he were saying: "Although He is the God of life and salvation and this is His proper work, yet, in order to accomplish this, He kills and destroys. These works are alien to Him, but through them He accomplishes His proper work. For He kills our will that His may be established in us. He subdues the flesh and its lusts that the spirit and its desires may come to life."[18]

The very indignation and resentment we harbor and/or express when we come up against the absolutely sovereign action of God in these matters indicates the truth of what is being said. The anger and indignation is the beginning of the suffering! Like Job we protest against God. Why? Because in actual suffering all theorizing is over. One enters into contention with God. Precisely in his rash protest over his suffering Job unwittingly speaks the truth about God.[19] In

---

18. LW 14.335.

19. I am indebted in this section to the fine essay by Klaus Schwarzwäller, "'Nun hat mein Auge dich gesehen' Leiden als Grundproblem der Theologie," in *Einfach von Gott reden: Festschrift für Friedrich Mildenberger zum 65 Geburtstag*, edited by Jürgen Roloff and Hans G. Ulrich (Stuttgart: Verlag W. Kohlhammer, 1994), 190-225. What was it that Job "saw" when God spoke to him out of the whirlwind that he had previously only "heard by hearing of the ear," so that he despised himself and repented in dust and ashes (Job 42:5-6)? Job had persistently held God to account in his protests over against his "comforters," who tried to exonerate God by their

his suffering he cries out to God as the ultimate answer to it all. As with Job, it is only through suffering that sinners come to know and speak such truth. As inveterate theologians of glory, we are bound to shy away from such truth and, like Job's friends, try to make excuses for God. We adjust our doctrine of God to fit our glory projects. If God doesn't "play fair," how can our works count? Thus do we render God innocuous by our flattery. Instead of being brought to the praise of God, we bend our efforts to justify him.[20]

True knowledge of God, therefore, does not come on a theological platter. We are predisposed to distort things, to see wrongly, and to speak falsely. We construct a doctrine of God amenable to our projects. So the only way to know God is through suffering, the suffering of the one who saves us. God, so to speak, has to get our attention so that we will see at last. Knowledge of God does not comprise sets of doctrinal truths that may be taken or left at our discretion, not even if those truths call themselves "A Theology of the Cross," which we subsequently take steps to put into practice. Whether *we* take it or whether *we* leave it makes no difference. As long as we think the matter is at *our* discretion, we remain the acting subjects. God is ultimately an insignificant cipher. There is no way through here. God can be known and had only through suffering

---

"theodicies." Job's friends thought his speech laying the responsibility on God was outrageous and blasphemous, but Job insisted on crying out against God since God is, according to "the hearing of the ear" (perhaps we might say "The Doctrine of God!"), the one who is supposed to be in charge. Now God, in declaring his awesome and universal majesty out of the whirlwind, actually approves what Job had said over against all the explanations of the "theologians." So God declares (42:7-9) that Job had spoken the truth, terrifying as it was and is. Job now *sees* that in the voice of his suffering he had unwittingly spoken the truth, and he is terrified by it: "I have uttered what I did not understand, things too wonderful for me which I did not know" (42:3). Job *sees* that through suffering the truth had literally been wrung out of him. He sees where previously he had heard and complained. He thus "despises himself and repents in dust and ashes."

20. See above, chap. 3, n. 7.

the divine deed of the cross. The cross does not merely inform us of something, something that may be "above," or "behind" it. It attacks and afflicts us. Knowledge of God comes when God happens to us, when God does himself to us. We are crucified with Christ (Gal. 2:19). The sinner, the old being, neither knows nor speaks the truth about God and consequently can only be put to death by the action of God. Such is the way one becomes a theologian of the cross, who can begin to speak and proclaim the truth of God, to "say what a thing is."[21]

21. The assertion that the truth about God is spoken out of suffering is common in Luther, sometimes in very radical form. In general it appears in the well-known insistence that God reveals himself "under the form of opposites" in weakness and suffering, or that God does his "alien work" of killing, afflicting, and bringing down to hell before he does his "proper work" of making alive, comforting, and raising to new life. Perhaps most radical are those instances where he speaks of God first becoming a devil for us before becoming God, and vice versa.

> Outwardly . . . grace seems to be nothing but wrath, so deeply is it buried under two thick hides or pelts. Our opponents and the world condemn and avoid it like the plague or God's wrath, and our own feeling about it is no different. Peter says truthfully [2 Pet. 1:19] that the Word is like a lamp shining in a dark place. Most certainly it is a dark place! God's faithfulness and truth always must first become a great lie before it becomes truth. The world calls this truth heresy. And we too are constantly tempted to believe that God would abandon us and not keep his Word; and in our hearts He begins to become a liar. In short, God cannot be God unless He first becomes a devil. All that God speaks and does the devil has to speak and do first. And our flesh agrees. Therefore it is actually the Spirit who enlightens and teaches us in the Word to believe differently. By the same token the lies of this world cannot become lies without first having become truth. The godless do not go to hell without first having gone to heaven. They do not become the devil's children until they have first been the children of God. (LW 14.31)

These strange words begin to yield some sense when one thinks as a theologian of the cross and "tells it like it is." Unconditional grace must first be an absolute threat to us as theologians of glory. There is no "cure" for the theology of glory. No mere "change" of mind or opinion is possible. Grace therefore can only appear as nothing but wrath. The executor of the wrath of God, however, is the devil. God therefore first becomes a devil. All that God says and does the devil must say and do first. One must first go to hell before one can be raised. There is no other way here. God must

THESIS 22. That wisdom which perceives the invisible things of God by thinking in terms of works completely puffs up, blinds, and hardens.[22]

---

be accorded the absolute right to do this. The sinner must suffer this if there is to be life.

More radical perhaps is a comment from the 1519-21 *Operationes in Psalmos* occasioned by Isa. 42:3, "A bruised reed he will not break and a dimly burning wick he will not quench."

> And I will say one thing more in my free and bold way. There are none nearer to God in this life than these haters and blasphemers of him, nor any sons more pleasing to him and beloved by him! And you can in this state make more satisfaction for sin in one moment than ever you could by repenting for many years together under a diet of bread and water. Hence it is true that in death (where this temptation prevails most), a Christian may in one moment get rid of all his sins, if he but act wisely under temptation. Here it is that those "groanings that cannot be uttered" are at work and prevail [Rom. 8:26]. (WA 5.170.25–5.171.3)

Remarkable passage! It makes no sense at all to a theologian of glory, but if we think of Job (above n. 19), for instance, it begins to make more sense. Like Job, the "blasphemer" at least does God the honor of acknowledging God as God. In extremity the sufferer is finally provoked enough, perhaps ultimately in death, to send complaint to the right address. Perhaps we can imagine God saying, "Ah, at last! I got you to talk to me! You spoke the truth about me in spite of yourself!" The promise is that he will not break the bruised reed nor quench the dimly burning wick. As with Job the situation is such that the suffering leads to truthful speech. No doubt Luther has Jesus' "blasphemy" in mind, the cry of dereliction from the cross. The theologian of glory always has great difficulty with that cry. In pious restraint the theologian of glory will refrain from such "blasphemy" and flatter God by absolving Him from all blame. But such pious speech simply robs God of the right to be God. So Luther could say that there are none closer to God in this life than "blasphemers," who at least do God the honor of letting Him be God!

22. Once again in the Latin the *intellecta conspicit* introduced in thesis 19 reappears. It is difficult to convey in English. I have tried to do it by speaking of a wisdom that perceives the invisible things of God via a scheme of works. The idea seems to be that the "wisdom" in question is what we have been speaking of all along as a false perception of the place of works. A theology of glory assumes that the invisible things of God are analogous to a scheme in which works count in the gaining of merit.

Thesis 22 marks the beginning of the next triad (22, 23, 24), which deals with the question of the wisdom of the law in the light of the great divide between the theologian of glory and the theologian of the cross. If, that is to say, the theologian of glory does not see God aright and thus speaks falsely, a false wisdom is the outcome. The wisdom guiding the theologian of glory is the wisdom of the law. The question here is what is the hold of such wisdom, religiously speaking, and what is the outcome? Thesis 22 speaks to the nature and hold of the wisdom of law and works; thesis 23 notes the consequences of the hold that law has on us; and thesis 24 raises the final question about the place and proper use of the wisdom of law by the theologian of the cross.

Thesis 22 is, in effect, a statement about the religious effect of the theology of glory and the wisdom of law upon which it is based. Religious people in particular seem to have difficulty being theologians of the cross. That is because the theology of the cross is quite devastating for our usual religious aspirations under the wisdom of law. The indignation and resentment against God spoken of above is aroused not only — perhaps not even principally! — because of the strenuousness and rigor of the life proposed, but finally because in the cross God has literally taken away from us the possibility of doing anything of religious merit. In Jesus God has cut off all such possibility. God, as St. Paul could put it, has made foolish the wisdom of the wise. We are rendered passive over against God's action. This is always galling for the old being. We adopt a very pious posture. It is, so the protests go, too easy, too cheap, it has no obvious ethical payoff, and so on and on. Religiously we like to look on ourselves as potential spiritual athletes desperately trying to make God's team, having perhaps just a little problem or two with the training rules. We have a thirst for glory. We feel a certain uneasiness of conscience or even resentment within when the categorical totality of the action of God begins to dawn on us. We are always tempted to return to the safety and assurance of doing something anyway. Generally, it is to be suspected, that is all we planned to do, a little something. But to surrender the "wisdom" of law and works, or better, to have it taken away, is the first indication of what it means to be crucified with Christ.

Thesis 22 takes aim particularly at our religious sensibilities, that uneasiness of conscience or feeling of resentment arising within us when our religious aspirations come under attack. The wisdom of our ordinary religious outlook, the scheme of law and works, simply puffs us up, blinds us, and hardens us. The theologian of glory becomes a "hater of the cross." In his proof for this thesis Luther picks up from the claim of the previous thesis that theologians of glory have reversed the value signs, calling the bad (works to gain merit) good and the good (suffering and cross) bad:

> Because men do not know the cross and hate it, they necessarily love the opposite, namely, wisdom, glory, power, and so on. Therefore they become increasingly blinded and hardened by such love, for desire cannot be satisfied by the acquisition of those things that it desires. Just as the love of money grows in proportion to the increase of money itself, so the dropsy of the soul becomes thirstier the more it drinks, as the poet says: "The more water they drink, the more they thirst for it." The same thought is expressed in Eccles. 1[:8]: "The eye is not satisfied with seeing, nor the ear filled with hearing." This holds true of all desires.
>
> Thus also the desire for knowledge is not satisfied by the acquisition of wisdom but is stimulated that much more. Likewise the desire for glory is not satisfied by the acquisition of glory, nor is the desire to rule satisfied by power and authority, nor is the desire for praise satisfied by praise, and so on, as Christ shows in John 4[:13], where he says, "Everyone who drinks of this water will thirst again."[23]

23. LW 31.53-54. "Dropsy" is a word for a malady that has disappeared from modern vocabulary. Ancients used it to designate accumulation of water or liquid in

What is interesting here is that Luther likens the plight of the theologian of glory to that of an obsessive lover or a miser. In our day the drug addict or alcoholic would be the closest parallel. The desire, the thirst for glory or wisdom or power or money, is never satisfied by the acquisition of what is desired. The more we get, the more we want. There is never real satisfaction, never the confidence that we have or have done enough. "How much money does it take to make one happy?" "Just a little more!" As sinners we are like addicts — addicted to ourselves and our own projects. The theology of glory simply seeks to give those projects eternal legitimacy. The remedy for the theology of glory, therefore, cannot be encouragement and positive thinking, but rather the end of the addictive desire. Luther says it directly: "The remedy for curing desire does not lie in satisfying it, but in extinguishing it."[24] So we are back to the cross, the radical intervention, end of the life of the old and the beginning of the new.

Since the theology of glory is like addiction and not abstract doctrine, it is a temptation over which we have no control in and of ourselves, and from which we must be saved. As with the addict, mere exhortation and optimistic encouragement will do no good. It may be intended to build up character and self-esteem, but when the addict realizes the impossibility of quitting, self-esteem degenerates all the more. The alcoholic will only take to drinking in secret, trying to put on the facade of sobriety. As theologians of glory we do much the same. We put on a facade of religious propriety and piety and try to hide or explain away or coddle our sins. In our day we will even curry affirmation and acceptance. We may listen to the voices that please us most, those of optimists who peddle "The Power of Positive Thinking," "Possibility Thinking," and similar

---

an organ or part of the body. Thus it became also a word for inordinate or insatiable thirst.

24. LW 31.54.

theological marshmallows. We may even be temporarily encouraged. But in more lucid moments, we, like the addict, suspect it won't do, that we aren't really up to it. Instead of building self-esteem the voices of optimism eventually undermine and weaken it. Ultimately they destroy (thesis 23).

As with the addict there has to be an intervention, an act from without. In treatment of alcoholics some would speak of the necessity of "bottoming out," reaching the absolute bottom where one can no longer escape the need for help. Then it is finally evident that the desire can never be satisfied, but must be extinguished. In matters of faith, the preaching of the cross is analogous to that intervention. It is an act of God, entirely from without. It does not come to feed the religious desires of the Old Adam and Eve but to extinguish them. They are crucified with Christ to be made new. But that is the subject of the next two theses.

THESIS 23. The law works the wrath of God, kills, curses, accuses, judges, and damns everything that is not in Christ.

Thesis 22 announced that the wisdom that thinks in terms of law and works is completely puffed up, blinded, and hardened. In other words, it always thinks of itself in glorious terms. The wisdom it espouses is the natural wisdom of the world. Thesis 23 announces flatly that in spite of all the glorious hot air, God is not ultimately interested in the law. The real consequence of such wisdom is laid bare: The law does not work the love of God, it works wrath; it does not give life (recall thesis 1!), it kills; it does not bless, it curses; it does not comfort, it accuses; it does not grant mercy, it judges. In sum, it condemns everything not in Christ. It seems an outrageous and highly offensive list. As Luther's proof quickly demonstrates, however, it comes right out of Paul in Galatians and Romans:

Thus Gal. 3[:13] states, "Christ redeemed us from the curse of the law" and "For all who rely on the works of the law are under the curse" [Gal. 3:10]; and Rom. 4[:15]: "For the law brings wrath"; and Rom. 7[:10]: "The very commandment which promised life proved to be the death of me"; and Rom. 2[:12]: "All who have sinned without the law will also perish without the law."[25]

The result of the clash between theses 22 and 23 is complete confusion. The wisdom of law puffs up, blinds, and hardens, but in so doing it kills and destroys. It is like a great balloon that ascends on the strength of its own hot air but finally goes too high into the stratosphere, bursts, and crashes to earth. Theologians of glory who operate according to the wisdom of law and works are eventually quite confounded. They are always tempted to place their trust in works. It is after all the only thing they know. At the same time they are perplexed and perhaps even attracted by radical attacks on such wisdom. Eventually antipathy to law is likely to set in. After all, they do not want to be "legalists"! They may, on occasion, even be worried about their own failure to live up to what the law demands. The usual defense of theologians of glory is to attempt some sort of accommodation, to water down the law in some way to make it less demanding. Trapped by the law, they can only become its secret enemy. Whether overtly or covertly, the only defense theologians of glory have against the destructive nature of law is some kind of antinomianism (anti-law-ism).

Antinomianism comes in many forms. The law will be rejected as old-fashioned or pietistic or fundamentalistic, or it will be contextualized or modified according to the latest scientific discovery or genetic theory, and so on. But then we are only delivered into the hands of a different fate, today usually some kind of genetic

25. LW 31.54.

determinism. The law doesn't let up, it only comes back in a different form. As Melanchthon said several times in the "Apology to the Augsburg Confession," "The Law always accuses."[26] "Therefore he who boasts that he is wise and learned in the law boasts in his confusion, his damnation, the wrath of God, in death."[27] In spite of our attempts to bring it to heel, the law all the while goes its way. There are no loopholes. It kills, curses, accuses, judges, and condemns. It is the first and cutting edge of the intervention from without into the closed cell of the addict. "The very commandment that promised life proved to be the death of me." But just at the end of the thesis there is a glimpse of hope that is destined to become clearer as we move into the final theses. The law condemns every-thing *that is not in Christ.* In Christ there is a way out.

THESIS 24. Yet that wisdom is not of itself evil, nor is the law to be evaded; but without the theology of the cross man misuses the best in the worst manner.

The negative assessment of the wisdom of law in theses 22 and 23, indeed, throughout the entire Disputation, is likely to make believers nervous. Is that wisdom evil in itself? As St. Paul could put it, "Is the law sin?" These questions flow finally into thesis 24, the last of those making up the keystone of the great arch. The "wisdom" of the law is not in itself evil. The theologian of the cross is not antinomian. Indeed, the theologian of the cross knows that only the crucified and risen Christ is the end of the law. The problem is in the fact that the theologian of glory *misuses* the wisdom of the

26. *The Book of Concord: The Confessions of the Evangelical Lutheran Church,* translated and edited by Theodore G. Tappert (Philadelphia: Fortress, 1959), 112.38, 125.128, 130.167.
27. LW 31.54-55.

law. What this thesis offers finally is the reason why wisdom and law have been given such a negative evaluation throughout. In themselves wisdom and law are entirely good, as are all of God's gifts. However, without the theology of the cross these gifts will simply be misused. Without the theology of the cross the sinner is of necessity bound to take credit for works and wisdom and therefore not to receive them as God's gifts.

It is necessary to get the full bite of this before moving to the final theses. The misuse of the wisdom of law is a matter of bondage. The sinner does not preside over this matter nor can the sinner make a free decision not to misuse the law and its wisdom. As we have seen, not even before the fall was there such active potency. So we could not simply say that this or that "correct theology" or proper instruction will remedy the matter. It is rather the burden of this thesis that *without the theology of the cross we misuse the best in the worst manner.* That is, unless we see everything through suffering and the cross and are led thereby to speak the truth, unless we are "brought low, reduced to nothing through the cross and suffering," we cannot but misuse and defile the gift of God in the worst way.[28] Without the theology of the cross we will of necessity take credit for works ourselves and place trust in them. Luther's proof puts the matter in no uncertain terms: "Whoever has been emptied through suffering no longer regards himself as the worker but rather God, who works and does all things in him."[29] Indeed, so removed is the theologian of the cross from worry about works, there is a kind of shocking indifference to the question as such:

> For this reason, whether God works or not is all the same to him. He neither boasts if he does works, nor is he disturbed if God does not work through him. He knows it is sufficient if he suffers

28. LW 31.55.
29. LW 31.55. I suggest a slightly different translation from LW 31.

and is brought low by the cross in order to be annihilated all the more.[30]

The point here is that the obsession for works as the basis for self-reliance is to be extinguished (thesis 22). God can even go the whole way. He can bring on the ultimate suffering of doing no works through believers in order to bring them lower still!

The last sentences of this proof represent the great turning to the concluding section of the Disputation. They indicate the final farewell to all that has gone before — the ineptitude of the law, the failure of the will, the blindness of sight, the false speaking, the misuse of wisdom — and open the way to the true righteousness worked by God's creative love. The final farewell is given in the words of John 3:7 spoken to Nicodemus who came seeking wisdom: "You must be born anew." We have arrived at that point now. No repairs, no improvements, no optimistic encouragements are possible. Just straight talk: "You must be born anew." But like Nicodemus we ask how that can be. Now all possibility is truly cut off. The theologian of glory, of course, will suggest one last stratagem: turn even that into something to do — perhaps crawling back into the womb to come out again. But therewith the insistence on doing something has at last turned into a cynical *reductio ad absurdum*. The theologian of glory has at last come up against something that can't be done! So Luther's proof executes the final *coup de grace* (literally: the stroke of grace!). "To be born anew, one must consequently first die and then be raised up with the Son of Man. To die, I want to emphasize, means to feel the very presence of death."[31]

One must first die and then be raised up with the Son of Man.

---

30. LW 31.55.

31. Again, I translate this differently from LW 31. Luther, it seems to me, wants to be more emphatic than LW 31 allows.

This is the gateway to the righteousness that avails before God. What are we to make of such dying? Like Nicodemus we will no doubt still ask, "How can these things be?" The theology of glory may still come up with something to do. Even a theology of the cross, as we have previously suggested, may be turned into a negative theology of glory. We may become an ascetic who comes as close to suicide as possible, or a flagellant, or a recluse, or hermit, or beggar, or embark on goodness knows what sort of way of self-appointed humiliation and suffering. Dying too can be taken on as a project. Sometimes in cults like that at Jonesville it becomes a horrible reality.

What does Luther intend by such constant talk of dying? Is it just a metaphor for conversion, or an analogy, a figure of speech perhaps, but not the real thing? The final sentence of the proof gives us a vital clue: "To die, I want to emphasize, means *to feel the very presence of death*." When readers come across this, they often exclaim that this seems too bland and mild after all the fuss up until now. Does it all boil down in the end to the mere "feeling" of death? Where is the *reality* of it all? It must be remembered here, however, that for Luther as for Paul the real "sting" of death was precisely in the way it "hits" us in soul and spirit. Thus, for Luther the sinner's experience of the terror of death is the real death. Actual physical death, even though sorrowful enough for loved ones, was in and of itself a much less serious matter.

Some passages from Luther illustrate this clearly. The first is from the *Lectures on Genesis* (22:11) occasioned by the sacrifice of Isaac. Abraham, Luther says, *actually* dies seven times because of his mental suffering over the demand to sacrifice his son.

> Natural death, which is the separation of the soul from the body, is simple death. But *to feel death, that is, the terror and fear of death — this indeed is real death*. Without fear death is not death; it is a sleep. As Christ says [John 11:26]: "He who believes in me will

not see death." For when fear has been removed, the death of the soul has been removed.[32]

The second is from a funeral sermon for the Elector, Duke John of Saxony. Luther speaks of the suffering and agony the duke experienced in making his confession before the Diet of Augsburg as his real death:

> We should therefore take comfort in the fact that Christ died and our beloved prince is caught up and fallen asleep in Christ's death and that he suffered a far more bitter death at Augsburg than now, a death that we are still obliged to suffer daily and incessantly from the tyrants and sectarians, and, indeed, also from our own conscience and the devil. *This is the real death.* The other physical death, when we pass away in bed, is only a childish death [Kindersterben] or animal death.[33]

The experience of the very presence of death, the sensing of its terror, is the real thing. Physical expiration is a lesser matter. A third passage, from the *Lectures on Romans,* where Luther is commenting on being baptized into the death of Christ (Rom. 6:3), declares that death in the real sense applies finally only to the death of sin and the sinner:

> [The good death] is the death of sin and the death of death, by which the soul is released and separated from sin and the body is separated from corruption and through grace and glory is joined to the living God. This is death in the most proper sense of the word, for in all other forms of death something remains that is mixed with life, but not in this kind of death, where there is the

32. LW 4.115 (emphasis mine).
33. LW 51.237-38 (emphasis mine).

purest life alone, because it is eternal life. For to this kind of death alone belong in an absolute and perfect way the conditions of death, eternal nothingness, and nothing will ever return from this death because it truly dies an eternal death. This is the way sin dies; and likewise the sinner, when he is justified, because sin will not return again for all eternity, as the Apostle says here, "Christ will never die again," and so forth [v. 9].[34]

So to die in this connection means to experience the very presence of death, to reach that point where the final intervention occurs, where one has "bottomed out." The theologian of glory finally is "frightened to death," if one may so speak. The terror is in the fact that the end of sin has come and the Old Adam and Eve can no longer survive. Then one is a candidate for being born anew. That is the gateway to being saved by the creative righteousness of God.

34. LW 25.310.

IV

God's Work in Us:
The Righteousness of Faith

THESES 25-28

We have arrived now at the other pier of the great arch spanning the way from the law of God to the love of God. Theses 25-28 set forth the life raised from the death spoken of at the conclusion of the proof for thesis 24. With that death the way has been cleared for God's work in us. Every other road, every other possibility, has been examined and rejected. The old self has the sickness unto death. There is no cure. Death is the end.

> **THESIS 25.** He is not righteous who works much, but he who, without work, believes much in Christ.

This thesis marks the final turn of the Disputation to the sole agency of the grace of God in the life of the theologian of the cross. It has been presupposed throughout and hinted at here and there, but now it comes out in the open. It still sounds rather exaggerated and offensive to our ears, but that is precisely the point. We have a hard time getting over the offense, and thus there is no letup, even here. The thesis is really nothing other than a statement of justification by faith alone without the deeds of the law. In fact, Luther quotes the Pauline passage (Rom. 3:20) to that effect in his proof. That doctrine is always a polemical doctrine and a permanent offense to the Old Adam and Eve. So when we arrive here at the end of the Disputation we should not and suddenly expect everything to "go soft." What is asserted here is precisely that God simply is not interested in works issuing out of the self's concern for its own righteousness. "Whatever is not of faith is sin." Only those who believe much in Christ are righteous before God, period. It always seems incredible to us, but getting used to that fact is what it means to die and be raised to newness of life in Christ, to be born anew. Only then will works that can be called "good" begin to be done. Good works, works done for the neighbor without calculation or claim, can begin when the Old Adam is put to death and the new appears.

Luther's proof is simply a bald assertion of the righteousness of faith based on passages from Romans. This, he remarks, is quite contrary to what we learn from Aristotle. "For the righteousness of God is not acquired by means of acts frequently repeated, as Aristotle taught, but it is imparted by faith, for 'He who through faith is righteous shall live' (Rom. 1[:17]) and 'Man believes with his heart and so is justified' (Rom. 10[:10])."[1] We don't get the bite of this unless we recall just what this reference to Aristotle means. Aristotle held that we acquire righteousness by doing righteous deeds, just as we acquire skills by practicing:

> Anything that we have to learn to do we learn by the actual doing of it: people become builders by building and instrumentalists by playing instruments. Similarly we become just by performing just acts, temperate by performing temperate ones, brave by perform-

1. LW 31.55.

ing brave ones. This view is supported by what happens in city states. Legislators make their citizens good by habituation; this is the intention of every legislator, and those who do not carry it out fail of their object.[2]

Aristotle sets forth commonsense human wisdom about good works. What he says certainly seems meet, right, and salutary. We learn to play the piano only by practicing, we learn a skill only by doing. This is the wisdom by which the world runs. It is what lawmakers try to inculcate. But not here. The righteousness before God comes only by hearing and believing. God *makes* us who we are (thesis 28!). Such righteousness can only appear absolutely shocking compared to the wisdom of an Aristotle. As we have seen throughout the Disputation, however, it could hardly be otherwise. Works performed on the premise that one was going to *become* righteous thereby are not good to begin with. They defend us against the goodness of God. They are done not for the neighbor but for the glory of the self. Works that can be called good, however, flow *from* righteousness as from an overflowing vessel, not into it as an empty one waiting to be filled. It is consequent then that the philosophical theses (which we are not commenting on here) are aimed at the Aristotelian premises undergirding a theology of glory. The first thesis (29) sets the stage: "Whoever wishes to apply himself to Aristotelian philosophy without danger to his soul must first be made truly foolish in Christ."[3] The cross has reversed everything. The foolishness of God in the cross is wiser than the wisdom of the world. The righteousness that avails before God is a being claimed by the crucified and resurrected Christ. It is not like accomplishing something but like dying and coming to life. It is not like earning something but more like falling in love. It is not the attainment of

2. Aristotle *Ethics* 92.
3. WA 1.355.1-2.

a long-sought goal, the arrival at the end of a process, but the beginning of something absolutely new, something never before heard of or entertained.

This means, of course, that the question of works that has plagued us throughout the Disputation must now finally be answered in an entirely different light. Once it is clear and actually believed that only we who "without works" believe much in Christ are righteous before God, once that preposterous joy actually hits us, a new day dawns. Such righteousness is simply complete in itself. It is like the joy and ecstasy of love. It is its own apology. It needs nothing. The way is cleared for *good* works. So in the proof for this thesis Luther could say,

> Therefore I wish to have the words "without work" understood in the following manner: Not that the righteous person does nothing, but that his works do not make him righteous, rather that his righteousness creates works. For grace and faith are infused without our works. After they have been imparted, the works follow.[4]

But Luther is very cautious. He wants to make absolutely certain that there be no confusion between the righteousness of faith and the works that will indeed follow. The works are in no way to be understood as the believer's own, but God's. The one justified by faith becomes Christ's vessel and instrument.

> Thus Rom. 3[:20] states, "no human being will be justified in His sight by works of the law," and, "For we hold that man is justified by faith apart from works of law" (Rom. 3[:28]). In other words, works contribute nothing to justification. Therefore he knows that works he does by such faith are not his but God's.

4. LW 31.55-56.

For this reason he does not seek to become justified or glorified through them, but seeks God. His justification by faith in Christ is sufficient to him. Christ is his wisdom, righteousness, etc., as 1 Cor. 1[:30] has it, that he himself may be Christ's vessel and instrument.[5]

Good works are God's work in the believer. They are something totally other than "works of law." The next thesis is designed to make this clear.

THESIS 26. The law says, "do this," and it is never done. Grace says, "believe in this," and everything is already done.

This thesis is quite incomprehensible to the theologian of glory. It seems at best an exaggeration and at worst just plain false. But the fact is that this negative judgment on the futility of the law is made from the vantage point of the theologian of the cross, being quite captivated by the grace of God. Looking back, we see that the law simply cannot bring into being what it commands. Furthermore, we see that whatever the law does bring into being bears no real relationship to what grace inspires. The law says, "Thou shalt love!" It is right; it is "holy, true, good." Yet it can't bring about what it demands. It might impel toward the works of law, the motions of love, but in the end they will become irksome and will all too often lead to hate. If we go up to someone on the street, grab them by the lapels and say, "Look here, you're supposed to love me!" the person may grudgingly admit that we are right, but it won't work. The results will likely be just the opposite from what our "law" demands. Law is indeed right, but it simply cannot realize what it

5. LW 31.56.

points to. So it works wrath. It can curse, but it can't bless. In commanding love law can only point helplessly to that which it cannot produce. So we repeat the paradoxical word of Leif Grane cited earlier, "What the Law requires is freedom from the law."[6] The law says, "Do this!" and it is never done.

This, Luther maintains in his rather short proof, is simply standard Pauline and Augustinian teaching: "The law works wrath and keeps all men under the curse."[7] Likewise, the second part of the thesis, "Grace says, 'believe in this,' and everything is already done," is straightforward Pauline and Augustinian fare. To extend the analogy of love, grace, instead of demanding love, simply gives it unconditionally. It is simply the "I love you." Faith justifies. Faith is the righteousness God wants and aims to get. Faith is what Adam and Eve lost, and faith is restored by grace alone. Luther backs this up by reference to St. Augustine: "'And the law (says St. Augustine) commands what faith obtains.' For through faith Christ is in us, indeed, one with us. Christ is just and has fulfilled all the commands of God, wherefore we also fulfill everything through him since he was made ours through faith."[8]

We should note that there is a certain exuberance in the language here. "Faith obtains" what law commands. Through faith Christ is in us. We fulfill everything through him since he was made ours through faith. The theologian of the cross simply will not back off from this and, when challenged, drives it home all the harder. To the theologian of glory the language seems utterly hyperbolic at best and at worst quite dangerous. What will happen to moral earnestness if people get wind of the claim that through faith all has been fulfilled in Christ? The temptation is always to fall back on the law, either in its original sense or perhaps in some new sense,

6. See "Introductory Matters," n. 21.
7. LW 31.56.
8. LW 31.56.

like a "third use." But the theologian of the cross knows that there is no way back. So Luther here pushes the language to the limit and will not back off. He knows that if there is faltering here, all will be lost. This is expressed nicely in a passage from Luther's 1519-21 *Operationes in Psalmos:*

> Wherefore, let this be your standard rule: wherever the holy scriptures command good works to be done, understand that it forbids you to do any good work by yourself, because you cannot; but to keep a holy Sabbath unto God, that is, a rest from all your works, and that you become dead and buried and permit God to work in you. Unto this you will never attain, except by faith, hope, and love; that is, by a total mortification of yourself (Col. 3:5) and all your own works.[9]

The insistence that only those works are truly good that are done spontaneously and joyously out of faith, hope, and love belongs to the very heart and soul of Luther's Reformation. That is why he can make the claim that faith doesn't have to be prompted to do good works because in faith everything is already done. This seems a preposterous claim. It is based, however, not on any claim we can make about ourselves but on the fact that the Christ who creates faith has fulfilled all things. Indeed, one should not miss the spectacular nature of the claim here. The believer is not being exhorted to do works on the basis of faith in order to catch up with what is demanded. Rather, the announcement is made that because the Christ who has fulfilled all things dwells within the person of faith, everything has *already* been done! There is simply nothing to do!

Here is a drastic parting of the ways with a theology of glory. The Christ of the cross *takes away* the possibility of doing something. The theologian of glory might be able to follow to the point of

9. Lenker, 277. WA 5.169.14-19.

accepting the truth that Christ has fulfilled all things, but then that will have to be used as motivational fuel to make sure the law gets its due. The point is precisely that the power to do good comes only out of this wild claim that everything has *already* been done. The language has to break out into preaching. Never mind that when we look to ourselves we find no sign of good works. Never mind our fears and anxieties. We are looking in the wrong place. Look to Christ! He has done it all. Nothing will be gained by trying to shore up the Old Adam. Christ leaves nothing for the Old Adam and Eve to do. The old can only be killed by the law, not given artificial respiration by recourse to it. That is the point of the language here and its exuberance. To the theologian of the cross the language of grace and faith must be pushed absolutely to this length — until it kills the old and raises the new. Nothing at all will ever be gained by backing down. We will only fall back into law where the demand continues endlessly and nothing is ever finally done. So we can only let the language of grace sound forth. Grace says, "believe it" and everything — EVERYTHING! — is already done. It is the creative Word of God. If that doesn't work then nothing will. The Disputation is moving inexorably to its concluding assertion about the creative love of God.

> **THESIS 27.** Rightly speaking, therefore, the work of Christ should be called the operative power, and our work, the operation; so our operation is pleasing to God by the grace of the operative power.

Thesis 27 spells out more directly what has been developed to this point. It is an attempt to describe how it all works for the life of faith. The real operative power in all works that can be called good is the work of Christ, that outrageous assertion that in Christ all that God demands has been fulfilled and that this Christ dwells in us by faith. The believer is "aroused" to work through living faith *in Christ's work,* to be "imitators" of God as Ephesians admonishes, "drawn" after Christ. That is the way the proof for this thesis puts it:

> Since Christ lives in us through faith, so he moves us to do good works through that living faith in his work, for the works that he does are the fulfillment of the commands of God given us through faith. If we look at them, we are moved to imitate them. For this reason the Apostle says, "Therefore be imitators of God as beloved children" [Eph. 5:11]. Thus deeds of mercy are aroused by the works through which he has saved us, as St. Gregory says: "Every act of Christ is instruction for us, indeed, a motivation." If his action is in us, it lives through faith, for it is exceedingly attractive according to the verse, "Draw me after you, let us make haste" [Song of Sol. 1:4] toward the fragrance "of your anointing oils" [Song of Sol. 1:3], that is, "your works."[10]

The entire passage deserves close attention. Notable is the fact that it says not one word about law. The impetus to good works comes entirely from being moved, aroused, and motivated by the completed work of the Christ, who dwells in the believer through faith. Christ's work is the complete fulfillment of the commands of God and as such moves the faithful to works. "Deeds of mercy are aroused by the *works through which he has saved us.*" The very action of Christ is in us through faith. It is "exceedingly attractive." The references to the Song of Solomon are not, of course, just incidental. There was, as is well known, a long tradition that interpreted this ancient biblical love song as an allegory of the relationship between Christ and his bride, the church. Without entering into that inter-

10. LW 31.56-57.

pretive quagmire, we can still remark how the language of faith mirrors the language of love. The language of law does not foster truly good works. The language of love is more appropriate. One is "drawn," "attracted" by the very action and saving works of Christ. It is, as pointed out above in the comment on thesis 26, the very claim that all has been fulfilled that draws the faithful to works. The language of love here already points to the final thesis about the creative power of divine love.

Christ is the "operator," the believer is the one "operated upon." The work thus produced is pleasing to God not in and of itself but by virtue of the grace of the operator, Christ. It is interesting and no doubt significant that the language used in this thesis *(opus operans, operatum, operis operantis)* comes from the sacramental vocabulary of medieval theology. Luther is no doubt thinking of the Augustinian insistence that Christ must first be a sacrament for us before he can be an example. So Christ is *operans*, the one doing the operating, and believers who receive his work sacramentally as sheer gift are *operatum*, worked upon. Their work in turn pleases God, not in and of itself, but *gratia operis operantis*, strictly because of the grace of Christ's operation. That is how it all works. This paves the way for the final move to the creative love of God.

THESIS 28. The love of God does not first discover but creates what is pleasing to it. The love of man comes into being through attraction to what pleases it.

Now we have arrived at the opposite side of the great arch described by the Disputation. All else has been shorn away, put to death. What remains is simply the creative love of God. The innermost nature of the operation of the previous thesis is now announced. It is love, the love of God that creates out of nothing, calls into being that which is from that which is not. This love of God that creates its object is contrasted absolutely with the love of humans. Human love is awakened by attraction to what pleases it. It must search to find its object and, one might add, will likely toss it aside when it tires of it.

The proof for this thesis Luther finds simply in the fact that the love of God flows forth to the unlovely:

> The first part [of the thesis] is clear because the love of God that lives in man loves sinners, evil persons, fools, and weaklings in order to make them righteous, good, wise, and strong. Rather than seeking its own good, the love of God flows forth and bestows good. Therefore sinners are attractive because they are loved; they are not loved because they are attractive. For this reason the love of man avoids sinners and evil persons. Thus Christ says: "For I came not to call the righteous but sinners" [Matt. 9:13].[11]

All of this flows forth strictly from the cross. It is the outcome of the *theologia crucis*:

> This is the love of the cross, born of the cross, which turns in the direction where it does not find good that it may enjoy, but where it may confer good upon the bad and needy person. "It is more blessed to give than to receive" [Acts 20:35], says the Apostle.[12]

Here we have reached the other side. God is not, as in the theology of glory, one who waits to approve those who have improved themselves, made themselves acceptable, or merited approval, but one who *bestows* good on the bad and needy. The great reversal is complete. Indeed, the final sentences of the proof touch in interesting fashion on a reversal in the very question of being itself:

11. LW 31.57.
12. LW 31.57.

Hence Ps. 41[:1] states, "Blessed is he who considers the poor," for the intellect cannot by nature comprehend an object that does not exist, that is, the poor and needy person, but only a thing that does exist, that is, the true and good. Therefore it judges according to appearances, is a respecter of persons, and judges according to that which can be seen, etc.[13]

The problem is that for a theology of glory the bad, poor, needy, or lowly cannot really exist. What really exists is the true, the good, and the beautiful, the great abstractions, the "invisible" things of God. Because the theologian of glory is always looking through what is actually given, the bad, poor, needy, and lowly are invisible. They don't show up on the scale of values and are not regarded. "Evil" is nonbeing. God has nothing to do with it. Hence, there is no reason why the Lord of all should condescend to them. But the Psalmist sees it otherwise, "Blessed is he who considers the poor."

Here at last the existential situation of the fallen creature, the sinfulness and need for salvation, is equated with the very question of being itself.[14] We get further insight into what it means to look on all things through suffering and the cross. Whereas the theologian of glory tries to see through the needy, the poor, the lowly, and the "nonexistent," the theologian of the cross knows that the love of God creates precisely out of nothing. Therefore the sinner must be reduced to nothing in order to be saved. The presupposition of the entire Disputation is laid bare. It is the hope of the resurrection. God brings life out of death. He calls into being that which is from that which is not. In order that there be a resurrection, the sinner must die. All presumption must be ended. The truth must be seen. Only the "friends of the cross" who have been reduced to nothing

13. LW 31.57-58.
14. See Vercruysse, "Gesetz und Liebe," 41-43, for some of these concluding insights.

are properly prepared to receive the justifying grace poured out by the creative love of God. All other roads are closed. The theologian of the cross is thus one who finally is turned about to see "the way things are."

Index of Names and Subjects

Index of Scripture References

Index of Scripture References

Printed in the United States
26355LVS00005B/334-339

9 780802 843456